WHAT DO YOU SEE?

Do You See A Young Woman or A Witch?

HOW TO RAISE YOUR
EXPECTATIONS
AND HOW TO SOLVE THE SUCCESS EQUATION

THE ULTIMATE, 45-DAY, QUICK-START GUIDE TO RAISING
YOUR EXPECTATIONS & ACHIEVING YOUR GOALS NOW!

Expectations

ISBN 979-8-9925935-5-6

TABLE OF CONTENTS

INTRODUCTION:

Is This a Book Worth Reading?

"Clay Clark's coaching has been tremendous. I can't say enough about it. He keeps me accountable. He keeps me focused on the business and implementing things that we need to work on to keep growing the business. When we first started working with you I had 4 employees and now I am up to ten employees and it is all because of the work we are getting now. We are getting more and more work."

- JAY POOLE

(Founder of the Seattle, Washington based Heating, Ventilation, and Air Conditioning business, AbsoluteHeatingCooling.com.)

"Five years ago, I just felt like we were stuck so I reached out to Clay Clark. Clay Clark helped me to build the systems we have now!"

- GABE SALINAS

(Founder of WindowNinjas.com)

"Clay, You've become an influencer. More than anything else you have evolved into an influencer where your word has more and more power. As you know there is alot of fake influencers out there. I'm glad that you and I agree so much. You are on it man! Everybody listen to this guy. He knows what he's talking about."

- ROBERT KIYOSAKI

(The best-selling author of The Rich Dad Poor Dad book series and a man who has sold over 40 million copies of his entrepreneur books.)

"We have grown 5X! We have grown from 60 to 300 employees. Before we teamed up with Clay Clark, we didn't have any systems or processes!"

- KEVIN THOMAS

(Founder of MultiClean.com)

"Clay Clark is an entrepreneur extraordinaire."

- DAVID ROBINSON

(NBA Hall of Fame Basketball Player, former NBA MVP, NBA Championship Winner & Investor.)

"Clay Clark has helped us to grow from 2 locations to now 6 locations. Clay has done a great job of navigating anything that has to do with running the business, building the systems, the checklists, the workflows, the audits, how to navigate lease agreements, how to buy property, how to work with brokers and builders. This guy is just amazing."

- CHARLES COLAW

(Co-Founder of ColawFitness.com. To see thousands of real business growth client success stories and case studies which Clay Clay has helped to produce since 2005 visit: www. ThrivetimeShow.com/Testimonials.)

"We've met some of the biggest CEOs in the world, guys that run the biggest Fortune 500 companies and Clay Clark has 100 times the backbone of the toughest person that you will see."

- ERIC TRUMP

(The Executive Vice President of The Trump Organization who is responsible for managing the $8 billion dollar business, thousands of employees, the Trump Organization's real estate and the Trump brands.)

"He's like Steve Martin meets Steve Forbes...I have known Clay Clark as a colleague for many years. He is among the most intentional, on task and on purpose people I know. We live in a world today that when it's all said and done, there's a lot said and very little done. Success in our personal and professional lives is not a product of what we wanted to do, hoped to do, or meant to do. Success is a direct result of what is actually done. Clay will help you set your course, and more importantly, take the steps you need to take to reach your destiny."

- JIM STOVALL

(Best-selling author, Founder and President of the Emmy Award winning Narrative Television Network, International Humanitarian of the Year, Founder and benefactor of the Stovall Center for Entrepreneurship at Oral Roberts University, Author of over 50 books (nine of which have become major motion pictures), A recipient of the U.S. Chamber of Commerce National Blue Chip Enterprise Award, An Emmy Award winner, An Oklahoma Hall of Fame inductee, An Emmy Award winner & One of the Ten Outstanding Young Americans awarded by the U.S. Jaycees.)

"He helped us to grow 4,000% from February to February! In the last two and a half days we have bettered our entire month of last year's February. The phone is blowing up. And everything is just blowing up! It's like a rocket ship and we are just pinching ourselves actually!"

- JULIANA GRIMNES

(Co-Founder of www.GiveADerm.com)

MICHAEL LEVINE

(The public relations expert of choice for 58 Academy Award winners, 34 Grammy Award winners, and 43 New York Times best-sellers, including Michael Jackson, Barbra Streisand and George Carlin shares his experience working with Clay Clark.)

"Over the last decade, Clay Clark has served—quite unintentionally, I suspect—as a corrective to our national epidemic of impatience. In an age of microwave ambitions and TikTok attention spans, Clay stands like a granite monument to that old-fashioned notion: sustained, unglamorous diligence. It is a principle he teaches not with the airy abstraction of a theorist but with the muscular conviction of a man who has lived it, bled for it, and—yes—prospered by it. He reminds us that excellence is never the result of a single, brilliant spasm but a symphony of disciplined habits conducted over years. Clay Clark has, in short, taught me that consistency is the ultimate disruptor.

What Clay embodies—and what he has impressed upon me repeatedly—is the radical idea that intentionality is not a slogan but a science. He is gloriously intolerant of drift, allergic to half-measures, and convinced (correctly) that success bends only to those who pursue it with a kind of cheerful relentlessness. Most mentors dispense platitudes about focus; Clay practices it, preaches it, and insists upon it with a vigor that borders on the evangelical. He has shown me that the future is not predicted; it is engineered. And the engineer, as Clay tirelessly argues, must rise every morning with the explicit intention to improve, to refine, to execute. Anything less is mere wishful thinking masquerading as ambition.

Over time—and here is the lesson that separates Clay from the common herd of motivational peddlers—he has demonstrated that diligence, practiced daily and without fanfare, compounds with the quiet ferocity of interest on a well-invested fortune. Clay has taught me that while talent glitters, diligence endures; while inspiration flickers, routine burns steadily; and while most men overestimate what one year can deliver, they catastrophically underestimate what ten years, guided by clear intent, can achieve. His stewardship of my thinking has been akin to intellectual weight training: repetitive, demanding, occasionally uncomfortable, and absolutely transformative.

And so, after a decade under his tutelage, I can say this without hesitation: Clay Clark is one of the rare figures in American entrepreneurial life who not only preaches the gospel of long-term intentionality but lives it with an almost monastic rigor. He has taught me the indispensable truth that greatness is not an accident, nor is it bestowed; it is built brick by tedious brick, day after unspectacular day—through the disciplined application of purpose.

In a culture drunk on shortcuts and intoxicated by instant gratification, Clay restores sanity. He restores proportion. And, in no small measure, he restores hope. If diligence and intentionality are indeed the twin engines of achievement, then Clay Clark is one of their most accomplished modern pilots.

One Entrepreneur vs. 24 Governors: Why Clay Clark Is Doing More for America's Growth by Michael Levine

In a nation obsessed with politics, it's worth asking a heretical question: who actually grows America's economy—career politicians or entrepreneurs who build, teach, and multiply businesses? By that measure, entrepreneurial guru **Clay Clark** may be more valuable to the nation's economic future than **24 state governors combined.**

Clark doesn't regulate, tax, or slow enterprise. He builds it. Through bestselling books, a widely followed podcast, live workshops, and daily content, Clark instructs **tens of thousands of entrepreneurs** on how to start, scale, and sustain profitable businesses. Each successful business creates jobs, pays taxes, innovates services, and strengthens local communities—without a single mandate or bureaucracy.

Contrast that with the reality in many states today. **Twenty-four governors**, aligned mainly with policies of over-regulation, punitive taxation, and compliance-first governance, have actively contributed to an environment where small businesses struggle to breathe. Excessive permits, rising labor mandates, energy costs, and tax burdens don't inspire growth—they suppress it. Entrepreneurs don't flee states because of "vibes"; they flee because math stops working.

Clark's value lies in leverage. One entrepreneur who teaches ten thousand others creates an exponential ripple effect. Governors, by contrast, often govern by restriction—measuring success by programs launched rather than businesses saved or jobs created.

America has never grown from the top down. It grows from the ground up—through risk-takers, builders, and educators who understand that prosperity is earned, not legislated. Clay Clark empowers the very people who fuel that engine.

In the long arc of economic impact, one pro-business educator multiplying entrepreneurs may outweigh two dozen governors slowing them down. That's not politics. That's arithmetic."

- MICHAEL LEVINE

(5X New York Times Best-Selling author and public relations expert of choice for 58 Academy Winner, 43 New York Times Best-Sellers 34 Grammy Award Winners and celebrities including: Michael Jackson, Barbara Streisand, George Carlin, Sam Kinison, Rodney Dangerfield and countless top level celebrities. Michael has been the PR consultant of choice for Pizza Hut, Mike, Nancy Kerrigan, Charlton Heston and countless other house-hold names and brands. Michael Levine has been referred to in different publications as the "Michael Jordan of entertainment P.R.)

CLIFTON TAULBERT

(The best-selling author, entrepreneur, and investor whose best-selling book was turned into the major motion picture, Once Upon a Time When We Were Colored (1989) shares his thoughts on Clay Clark.)

"Clay Clark has been recognized nationally by the White House as Oklahoma's Small Business Entrepreneur of the Year, and he still hasn't reached the seasoned age of forty. He has learned to leverage his business acumen and now finds himself in multiple successful business partnerships. So I was not surprised at all when he set out to launch Thrive15.com – the place to get what you need to know to get you where you want to go. Those are his words. This book extends his winning talks beyond sold-out conferences to an audience of thousands more nationwide and around the world. And through Thrive15.com, he will open up passageways for others to live beyond the "just surviving" mentality. He celebrates success wherever it is found. He understands the hard work and dedication required. He really does admire Napoleon Hill and fills his life with Mr. Hill's actionable quotes. They are all through this book. As I look at Clay's success and his larger-than-life vision for his future, he is well on his way to emulating the man he so admires. And quite frankly, he is placing him in a similar position to be admired and quoted as his life and businesses continue to THRIVE. Oftentimes people offering advice simply trust that the message is understood and move on, but not Clay Clark. He is committed to being in your face for your success. Not afraid of repetitious conversation and in-your-face humor, he is committed to each reader getting the message and more importantly, implementing the action steps set forth in this book and those voiced at Thrive15.com. Embracing and implementing the action steps in his books and training. Clay Clark is obsessed with implementing the action steps around your "big idea." This man gets emotional over your business success – maximizing your talents and potential. He remembers his dorm-room start and fully celebrates yours. Quoting Clay, "My friend, as you can tell by now, running a successful business is about so much more than just having a 'big idea'.

Your BIG IDEA is important, but the overwhelming majority of what will make your business succeed or fail has little to do with the 'big idea itself and everything to do with the execution of the 'big idea.'" Clay leaves us no doubt that action on our part matters. His life as well as his insightful consulting encounters become a clear window through which we can look and see what is possible in many of our lives if we are willing to put in the time and effort necessary to turn ideas into reality. Clay clearly points out that our "want to" becomes the driver of our actions or lack of actions. Yes, I could have failed had I not embraced the notion that execution of a plan matters. Clay is right. His life challenges us to not settle, but to THRIVE. In doing so, we place ourselves in a position to light the darkness for others. It is in our reach to others that we truly maximize our existence on this planet. If I were still home in the Delta doing the same thing all those around me were doing, I seriously doubt that I would be able to light the pathway for myself or others. Today I am lighting the darkness as a businessman and writer, telling others what is possible for their lives. Clay's passionate plea for others to move beyond merely surviving comes from an honest place of caring. Why fail when you can THRIVE? Thank you, Clay, for not being afraid to step out beyond the ordinary and for inviting us along on your remarkable journey."

– CLIFTON L. TAULBERT

"We definitely feel the growth. It's been amazing. Clay Clark has really helped us to expand. It was scary at first. I know I needed someone to guide us through this, through employees, through income, through spending. There are a lot of problems when you have a business and you can become very overwhelmed very fast. It's the best decision we've ever made!"

- GINNY MINGIONI

(Co-Founder of NewConcept.Healthcare. To see thousands of real business growth client success stories and case studies which Clay Clay has helped to produce since 2005 visit: www. ThrivetimeShow.com/Testimonials.)

"5 years ago, we were stuck so I reached out to you guys. You helped me build the systems we have now. I always had coaches and I knew that I wasn't going to grow my business without a proven coach and now I'm a success story (with 11 locations). Clay was able to help us develop processes for everything that happens within the business going down the line from how to answer phones to how to generate leads to checklists."

- GABE SALINAS

(Founder of WindowNinjas.com. To see thousands of real business growth client success stories and case studies which Clay Clay has helped to produce since 2005 visit: www. ThrivetimeShow.com/Testimonials.)

Why Does Inc. Magazine Report That "Why 96 Percent of Businesses Fail" by Default?

READ - *https://www.inc.com/bill-carmody/why-96-of-businesses-fail-within-10-years.html*

Why Is Only .00108% of the U.S. Population Successful by Default?

What Are Your Chances of Succeeding in Business by Default?

* According to www.USDebtClock.org, as of June 18, 2025, the population of the United States is 341,865,993, and just 9,282,734 Americans are self-employed.

* 2.71% of the United States population is self-employed.

* According to www.Inc.com, "96% of businesses fail."

* By default only 371,309 Americans will build a successful business.

Why are 73.6% of adults in the United States now classified as being overweight or obese based upon their actual Body Mass Index (BMI), according to the Centers for Disease Control?

READ - *https://www.cdc.gov/nchs/fastats/obesity-overweight.htm*

Think about these numbers DEEPLY and ask yourself, why? Why is just .00108% of the U.S. population successful in business by default? If just .00108% of the population is successful by default, why do Doctor Zoellner and I just keep winning over and over again? Why do the long-time clients and the founders of www.ColawFitness.com, Amber and Charles Colaw, stay in such great physical shape? How does the long-time client and the founder of www.KvellFit.com maintain such a high-level of fitness?

Why are 73.6% of adults in the United States now classified as being overweight or obese based upon their actual Body Mass Index (BMI), according to the Centers for Disease Control, while my personal trainer, Colton Claussen is a lean and fit muscle-building machine?

Is it Colton's genetics that allow him to maintain his muscular build? Is it my super paleness that allows me to succeed in business? Was I raised with money? No. Did I have a wildly successful family member who invested financially in my success? No. Am I a genius? No. I took algebra multiple times unsuccessfully, yet I keep succeeding in business year after year and decade after decade. In fact, as of the time I am writing this, I've been self-employed for 29 years.

Pictured from left to right: Laya Clark, Havana Clark, Doctor Robert Zoellner, Amy Zoellner, Santa Claus, Vanessa Clark, Clay Clark, Aubrey Napoleon-Hill Clark, Angelina Clark and Scarlett Clark. Between Doctor Zoellner and I, we have been able to found / co-found many multi-million dollar companies including (Alphabetically speaking): AtoZMM.com, DJConnection.com, DrZoellner.com, EITRLounge.com, EpicPhotos.com, FearsClark.com, MakeYourDogEpic.com, MakeYourLifeEpic.com, Party Perfect Rentals, The Tulsa Bridal Association Wedding & Bridal Show, Tip Top K9 Franchising, Z66AA.com, Etc.)

Although Doctor Zoellner and I both grew up without money, we have done well financially in a diverse variety of industries. Why? Why do we both experience tremendous success time and time again in many different industries? Is it genetics? Is it luck? He worked at a Mexican restaurant to pay his way through college. I worked at Applebee's, Target and DirecTV to fund and build my first successful business, www. DJConnection.com. Why have Doctor Zoellner (who I often host on the www.ThrivetimeShow.com Business Podcast) and I been able to achieve success in the following industries and more when only .00108% of the United States population is successful by default?

Accounting	Awards and Trophy Sales	Business Coaching / Consulting
Apartment Rentals	Bakeries for Cookies	Business Evaluation
Apparel	Bakeries for Cheesecakes	Cabinet Building
Appliance Sales		Calibration Shops
Architects	Bakeries for Wedding Cakes	Call Centers
Audio / Visual	Banking	Car Wash
Auto Auctions	Baseball Coaching	Carpet Cleaning
Auto Dealership	Basketball Coaching	Chiropractic
Auto Detailing	Beauty College	Church Growth
Auto Lift	Beauty Salon	Cleaning Service
Auto Parts	Book Writing	Concrete
Auto Wrap	Bridal Shows	Concrete / Decorative Flooring
Autobody Repair	Bridal Stores	Concrete / Pumping
Automotive Repair		

- Cosmetic Surgery
- Counseling
- Cyber Security
- Dent Repair
- Dentistry
- Dermatology
- Disk Jockeys
- Document Shredding
- Dog Boarding
- Dog Breeding
- Dog Grooming
- Dog Training
- Doors and Windows
- Dumpster Rentals
- Engineering
- Excavation Electrical
- Executive Coaching
- Eyelash Extensions and Permanent Makeup
- Family Medical Clinics
- Fencing
- Fitness Gyms
- Fitness via Group Training and Classes
- Fitness via Personal Training
- Fitness via Pilates

- Flooring- Carpet Installation
- Functional Medicine
- Fundraising
- Funeral Homes
- Furniture Sales
- Garage Door Repair
- Glass Block Sales
- Government Contracting
- Gutters
- Gymnastics and Tumbling
- Haircuts
- Handyman / Home Maintenance and Repair
- Hardware Stores
- Health Supplements
- Heating, Ventilation, and, Air Conditioning (HVAC)
- Home Automation
- Home Building
- Home Restoration
- Home Remodeling
- Information Technology Support
- Insulation and Wall Foam

- Insurance Sales
- Interior Design
- In-Store Retail
- Investor Relations / Financial Planning
- Janitorial Services
- Jewelry
- Laboritory Consulting
- Landscaping
- Lawn Care
- Legal (Law Firms)
- Log Cabin Supplies
- Manufacturing
- Marina Rental / Sales
- Marketing
- Martial Arts
- Medical
- Medical Research
- Ministry
- Monogram
- Musician / Singer / Songwriter
- Music School
- Mortgage Sales
- Nursery / Landscape Supplies
- Online Retail / Product Sales

Optometry

Ophthalmology

Outdoor Living

Outdoor Signage

Orthodontics

Pest Control

Personal Training

Phone Repair

Phone Sales

Photography

Photography- Commercial Photography

Photography- Real Estate Photography

Photography- Wedding Photography

Physical Therapy

Plumbing

Podcast Production

Pool Builders

Pool Installation / Construction

Pool Maintenance / Pool Supplies

Plumbing

Precious Metals

Professional Hockey

Professional Sports

Property Management

Public Relations

Public Speaking

Real Estate

Real Estate Agents

Real Estate Appraisal

Remodeling and Construction

Resort Management

Restaurants

Retirement Homes

Roofing

RV Parks

School and Private School Marketing

Security Systems and Alarms

Skin Care

Slab Installation

Shared Office Space

Staffing

Song-Writing

Spa / Medical Spa

Spine Surgery

Tours

Trailer Sales

Transportation and Shuttle Services

Tree Removal

Tutoring

Vacation and Scuba Diving

Vacation Planning

Vacation Rentals

Videography

Water Purification

Window Cleaning

Window Repair

Wood Floor Inspection

Yacht Rentals

Youtube Influencer

Having worked with thousands of great people like you to help start and grow super-successful businesses, I know that if you have the mental capacity and tenacity needed to read this book, you too can learn how to become successful. However, we can all choose to learn from either mentors or mistakes. On behalf of your wallet, your life, your net worth, and your future success, I HIGHLY RECOMMEND that you choose to learn from mentors.

NOTABLE QUOTABLE

"No one lives long enough to learn everything they
need to learn starting from scratch. To be successful,
we absolutely, positively have to find people who have
already paid the price to learn the things that we need to
learn to achieve our goals."

- BRIAN TRACY

(Legendary best-selling author, trainer, speaker and investor.)

NOTABLE QUOTABLE

"I don't claim to be a fitness expert, but I do know that
most people are not in great physical shape by default.
Is it the school system's fault? Is it our culture's fault?
Is it the food industry's fault? I don't claim to have all of
the answers, but I do know that it is totally possible for
you to get in the best shape of your life if you are simply
willing to schedule time to workout with a trainer or a
group class while becoming intentional about what you
are eating on a daily basis."

- COLTON CLAUSSEN

(The Founder of www.ClaussenTulsaPersonalTraining.com)

You can achieve your goals faster, and you prevent your life
from becoming a time- and money-wasting disaster when you
choose to learn from a proven mentor.

When I drive my vehicle from point A to point B (in my
oversized and heavily dented white van with 160,000 miles on
it), I choose to use a GPS (Global Positioning System) rather
than attempting to navigate to the desired location based upon
my shadow, my location in relation to the sun, or the feelings
I have. I do not aspire to become a modern-day Magellan by
plotting my course based upon my ever-expanding knowledge
of geography. I would rather trust a proven system.

When I was working at Applebee's, Target and DirecTV in an attempt to fund the growth of my first successful business and what would become one of America's largest wedding entertainment companies (DJConnection.com), I was obsessed with finding the best way to do everything. From the time I started DJConnection at the age of 15 (under the name C&G DJ Service) until I sold the business I was obsessed with saving time by learning and applying success systems and proven processes that would help me grow the business. Thus, when I was 20 years old I was named by the Tulsa Metro Chamber of Commerce as the Entrepreneur of the Year and when I was 27 I was named by the United States Small Business Administration as Oklahoma's Young Entrepreneur of the Year. In order to achieve rapid growth, I hired the best disk jockeys I could find, trusted lighting experts, audio experts, proven advertisement consultants, world-class branding experts and even the exact same marketing team that was working directly with the country music star Garth Brooks and other big-time brands. Why would I spend all of that money on hiring experts? Because I didn't hate myself enough to NOT hire people that knew the proven path that I needed to follow in order to create a world-class brand and industry leader. Was it expensive to hire experts that knew what they were doing? No. It was expensive to NOT hire people that knew what they were doing because we can all either learn from mentors or mistakes.

NOTABLE QUOTABLE

"The successful leader must plan his work, and work his plan. A leader who moves by guesswork, without practical, definite plans, is comparable to a ship without a rudder. Sooner or later he will land on the rocks. One of the penalties of leadership is the necessity of willingness, upon the part of the leader, to do more than he requires of his followers. Efficient leadership calls for ability to organize and to master details. No genuine leader is ever "too busy" to do anything which may be required of him in his capacity as leader. When a man, whether he is a leader or follower, admits that he is "too busy" to change his plans, or to give attention to any emergency, he admits inefficiency. The successful leader must be the master of all details connected with his position."

– NAPOLEON HILL

(The best-selling author of Think and Grow Rich. I named my son Aubrey Napoleon-Hill Clark after Napoleon-Hill because Napoleon Hill's research, teaching and writing had such a profound impact on me and my wife.)

NOTABLE QUOTABLE

"A Carnegie or a Rockefeller or a James J. Hill or a
Marshall Field accumulates a fortune through the
application of the same principles available to all of us,
but we envy them and their wealth without ever thinking
of studying their philosophy and applying it to ourselves.
We look at a successful person in the hour of their
triumph and wonder how they did it, but we overlook
the importance of analyzing their methods, and we
forget the price they had to pay in the careful and well-
organized preparation that had to be made before they
could reap the fruits of their efforts."

– NAPOLEON HILL

*(The best-selling author of Think & Grow Rich and the number
one best-selling self-help author of all time.)*

NOTABLE QUOTABLE

"Our greatest weakness lies in giving up. The
most certain way to succeed is always to try just
one more time."

- THOMAS EDISON

*(The American inventor and businessman who founded General
Electric. During Thomas Edison's career he developed electric
power generation, sound recording, and motion pictures. Think
about how different the world would be if he had not maintained
his persistence to develop the first functional and practical
lightbulb, recorded sound and recorded audio.)*

FUN FACTS

During Benjamin Franklin's Life He Invented

the Following Items and More:

1. The Franklin Stove

2. Bifocals

3. The Rocking Chair

4. Flexible Catheter

5. The Lighting Rod

Benjamin Franklin's 13 Virtues:

1. **Temperance:** Eat not to dullness; drink not to elevation.

2. **Silence:** Speak not but what may benefit others or yourself, avoid trifling conversation.

3. **Order:** Let all your things have their places; let each part of your business have its time.

4. **Resolution:** Resolve to perform what you ought; perform without fail what you resolve.

5. **Frugality:** Make no expense but to do good to others or yourself; waste nothing.

6. **Industry:** Lose no time; be always employed in something useful; cut off all unnecessary actions.

7. **Sincerity:** Use no harmful deceit; think innocently and justly; and if you speak, speak accordingly.

8. **Justice:** Wrong none by doing injuries or omitting the benefits that are your duty.

9. **Moderation:** Avoid extremes; forebear resenting injuries so much as you think they deserve.

10. **Cleanliness:** Tolerate no uncleanness in body, clothes or habitation.

11. **Tranquility:** Be not disturbed at trifles, nor at accidents.

12. **Chastity:** Be chaste in matters with the opposite sex.

13. **Humility:** Imitate Jesus and Socrates.

When I wanted to learn how to master the art of public relations, I hired Michael Levine, the best public relations expert that the modern world has given us. Why? Michael Levine was and is a master of public relations, and I would rather pay Michael Levine and learn from mentors than from mistakes. In fact, Michael Levine is a best-selling author of books on public relations including *Guerrilla P.R.*; he has represented 58 Academy Award winners, 34 Grammy Award winners, and 43 New York Times best-sellers, including Michael Jackson, Prince, Barbra Streisand, George Carlin, Charlton Heston, David Bowie, Michael J. Fox, and many other household names. Was it monetarily expensive to hire Michael Levine? Yes. However, it was too expensive to not have the wisdom and training that Michael Levine provided, because we can all either learn from mentors or mistakes. Learn more about Michael Levine today at: www.BoundlessMediaUSA.com

When I am renovating an investment property or building a property from the ground up, I choose to hire highly skilled contractors rather than trying to learn how to become a master carpenter, expert tile-guy and plumbing extraordinaire. As I write this right now, I am in the process of renovating a ranch, building a cabin and looking to buy more lakeshore properties in order to build yet another investment property. Am I going to learn all of the trades needed to build another lake-view vacation rental? No. So I am going to walk over to my neighbor's house and I am going to ask him who built his amazing house. Why? Because I do not hate myself enough to attempt to learn everything from scratch. Then I will hire a proven builder to build the house I want.

When I wanted to learn how to organize my day, manage my time, and scale an organization, I tirelessly worked to schedule an opportunity to shadow and follow the CEO of QuikTrip, Chet Cadieux, and the founder of Hobby Lobby, David Green. Was it difficult and expensive to make the connections needed to schedule these opportunities to learn from the men leading billion-dollar companies? No. It is difficult to NOT learn from men leading billion-dollar companies. My friend, we can all either learn from mentors or mistakes. Learn more about QuikTrip and Hobby today at:www.QuikTrip.com and www.HobbyLobby.com. As a fun twist of fate, just yesterday the founder of Hobby Lobby's public relations reached out to us to schedule him to be another expert guest on the www.ThrivetimeShow.com podcast.

When I am writing and recording a song, I hire a highly skilled producer to clean up and master the vocals rather than attempting to become the modern Quincy Jones, Dr. Dre., Timbaland and Rick Rubin of my generation. Why? Because I want to spend my energy on writing melodies, big choruses, lyrics, and songs that mean something; I don't want to spend my day putting in the thousands of hours it would take to become the next super-producer like Babyface or Jon Bellion.

When I decided to start investing in gold and silver on a consistent basis as a way to protect my wealth against the financial erosion caused by inflation, I hired Andrew Sorchini and his team at www.BH-PM.com. I didn't hire Andrew Sorchini because I wanted to buy precious metals from somebody based in Beverly Hills; I hired him because a man I know who owns a bank and who I have trusted for over 15 years told me that Andrew Sorchini was his precious metals dealer of choice. Does Andrew Sorchini make a commission to buy and sell gold? Yes. Is it expensive to buy precious metals from Beverly Hills Metals, Andrew Sorchini & www.BH-PM.com? No. It's expensive to run around the world attempting to become a precious metals expert while buying precious metals from hacks, hucksters, scammers, and the many scamming jackasses that are commonly found within many industries.

Pictured above is the founder of BH-PM.com (Beverly Hills Precious Metals) Andrew Sorchini, Eric Trump and Lin Sorchini. This photo was taken in my office during a business conference that both Andrew Sorchini and Eric Trump were speaking at.

Pictured above is Lin Sorchini, General Michael Flynn and the founder of BH-PM.com (Beverly Hills Precious Metals) Andrew Sorchini. This photo was taken backstage during one of the conferences that I was hosting featuring General Flynn, Eric Trump, Andrew Sorchini and other subject matter experts and speakers.

NOTABLE QUOTABLE

"I believe that health is your ultimate wealth. It doesn't matter how much money you make if you are dead. It doesn't matter how much money you make if your body is falling apart due to poor health. As a personal trainer, I have worked with big-time professionals and high net worth individuals, and I can tell you whether you want to make more money or you want to get into the best shape of your life. The clients that achieve the most success in their fitness and financial journey all have a proven mentor and personal trainer to guide them, to coach them, and to hold them accountable."

- COLTON CLAUSSEN

(The Founder of www.ClaussenTulsaPersonalTraining.com)

When I wanted to start the Midwest's most successful photography company, I chose to invest large sums of money into hiring highly skilled photographers who could teach me and my team how to provide world-class photography to the brides and grooms we worked with, while scaling EpicPhotos. com. Was it expensive to hire Derek Scott and Corey Lack to help teach myself and my team how to offer world-class photography to our customers? No. It's expensive to NOT learn photography from photography experts, because we can all either learn from mentors or mistakes. Learn more about Derek Scott and Corey Lack's photography services today by hunting around the internet or visiting:

www.CoreyLackPictures.com

Think about this for a second. I started one of the nation's most successful wedding photography companies with no skills in the world of photography, and I started one of the Midwest's most successful haircut chains without having any skills in the area of men's hair. How? I chose to learn from mentors and not mistakes. When I wanted to master search engine optimization, online advertising, and marketing, I hired the "The Father of Search Engine Optimization," Bruce Clay, to teach me how search engines work and how to build fully search engine optimized websites. Was it expensive? No. It's expensive to NOT pay the $8,000 per month needed to hire Bruce Clay to teach me search engine optimization, because we can all choose to either learn from mentors or mistakes. Learn more about Bruce Clay today at www.BruceClay.com or by purchasing a copy of *Search Engine for Dummies*, which he wrote.

Today as I am writing these very words, I am using the legal services of www.WintersKing.com to help me nail down the details on three business deals I am working on. Why? Because I don't hate myself enough to NOT hire top legal counsel to help me write up big-time agreements for big-time projects that I am working on. Although I grew up poor, I chose not to remain poor. A big reason that I am always able to achieve massive success is because I am constantly choosing to learn from mentors and not from mistakes. Why did I choose www.WintersKing.com to help me handle the legal aspects of my business? Because Tom Winters, Mike King, Wes Carter, and the www.WintersKing.com team have worked with hugely successful authors, influencers, and business people, including Pastor Craig Groeschel, Joel Osteen, Donald Trump Jr., Eric Trump, and countless other big-time authors and brands. Because I do not hate myself, I have chosen to hire the best and not the amateur hour. Is it expensive to hire www.WintersKing.com? No. It's expensive to NOT hire www.WintersKing.com. I cannot imagine the legal jackassery I would be dealing with if I hired an attorney who did not know what they were talking about, or if I had chosen to hack away on legal documents myself. Do I get paid commissions to recommend www.WintersKing.com? No. But I have asked...and legally they cannot pay me copious amounts of commissions.

Hopefully, I have clearly established the concept and best practice belief that it is better to learn from mentors than from mistakes. If you insist on working based upon guesswork and sprinting through the minefield of life hoping to find your lucky lottery ticket to success, I can't help you. But if you want to know the most direct and proven path to learn how to start and grow a super successful business, then this book is for you.

Tom Winters, Eric Trump, (my incredible wife) Vanessa Clark & I celebrate the combined effort it took to get Eric Trump's book Under Siege to become a New York Times #1 Best-Selling Non-Fiction Book. My team and I designed the book cover, introduced Eric to Tom Winters and his literary legal team and worked relentlessly to push the book into existence and to diligently edit the book.

NOTABLE QUOTABLE

"In the absence of processes that guide people, experienced people need to lead and do everything. But in established companies where much of the guidance to employees is provided by proven processes and is less dependent upon managers with detailed hands on experience, then it makes sense to hire or promote somebody or someone who needs to learn from experience."

- CLAYTON CHRISTENSEN

(Best-selling author and renowned Professor of Business Administration at the Harvard Business School who was regarded as one of the world's top experts on innovation and growth. To hear Clayton Christensen's interview with Clay Clark, visit ThrivetimeShow.com.)

NOTABLE QUOTABLE

"Resources are what he uses to do it, processes are how he does it, and priorities are why he does it."

- CLAYTON M. CHRISTENSEN

(The legendary Harvard Business professor, www. ThrivetimeShow.com guest and best-selling author.)

NOTABLE QUOTABLE

"If you can't describe what you are doing as a process, you don't know what you're doing."

- W. EDWARDS DEMING

(American business theorist, composer, economist, industrial engineer, management consultant, statistician, and writer.)

Where Can You Find Proven Mentors?

Every successful person that I have ever met has more money than time, thus, they are typically not found shaking hands at luncheons, or networking at your local Chamber of Commerce trying to convince you to join their next 'can't miss' multi-level program. Super successful people are typically found leading their organizations, growing their businesses, and pursuing their goals. This is exactly why I started the 2-Day Interactive www.ThrivetimeShow.com Business Growth Conferences and the www.ThrivetimeShow.com podcast 4,000 + episodes ago. I wanted to provide access for myself and great people like you to the life-changing wisdom, proven processes and systems provided by super successful people so that you and I could choose to learn from mentors rather than mistakes.

Listed Below Is a Partial List of ThrivetimeShow.com Guests:

 The co-founder of Square, **Jim McKelvey**.

 Celebrity Chef, Entrepreneur, and *New York Times* Best-Selling Author, **Wolfgang Puck**.

 Senior Editor for Forbes and 3x Best-Selling Author, **Zack O'Malley Greenberg**.

 International best-selling author, investor and podcaster, **Robert Kiyosaki**.

 Heisman Award-winning football player turned entrepreneur and philanthropist, **Tim Tebow**.

 Legendary Former Key Apple Employee Turned Venture Capitalist, and Best Selling Author, **Guy Kawasaki**.

 Senior pastor of the largest church in America with over 100,000 weekly attendees (Lifechurch.tv), **Craig Groeschel**.

 NBA Hall of Famer, 2-time NBA Champion, and 2-time Gold Medal Winner, **David Robinson**.

 Honest Tea Founder, **Seth Goldman**.

 Former CEO of YUM! (A&W Restaurants, Taco Bell, Pizza Hut, KFC) During Novak's Tenure at Yum! Brands, the company doubled the number of restaurants to 41,000, market capitalization grew to almost $32 billion from just under $4 billion and it was an industry leader in return on invested capital, **David Novak**.

The iconic comedian, actor, standup comedian and former Saturday Night Live cast member, **Jim Breuer**.

 8x *New York Times* Best-Selling Author and Leadership Expert, **John Maxwell**.

 One of the Most Downloaded Business Podcasters of All-Time (EOFire.com), **John Lee Dumas**.

 PR consultant of choice for Michael Jackson, Prince, Nike, Charlton Heston, Nancy Kerrigan, etc., **Michael Levine.**

 One of America's most trusted financial experts who has written nine consecutive *New York Times* bestsellers with 7 million+ books in print, **David Bach**.

 New York Times Best-Selling Co-Author of *Rich Dad Poor Dad*, **Sharon Lechter**.

 Assistant to the President, Director of Trade and Manufacturing Policy, and the national Defense Production Act policy coordinator, **Peter Navarro**.

 Former National Security Advisor of the United States, **General Flynn**.

 MyPillow.com founder, **Mike Lindell**.

 New York Times Best-Selling Author of Contagious: Why Things Catch On and Wharton Business Professor, **Jonah Berger**.

 New York Times Best-Selling Author of Made to Stick and Duke University Professor, **Dan Heath**.

 The *New York Times* bestselling author of *The Subtle Art of Not Giving a F$%k*, blogger and investor, **Mark Manson**.

The author of the *New York Times* bestsellers *The 48 Laws of Power*, *The Art of Seduction*, *The 33 Strategies of War*, *The 50th Law*, *Mastery* and *The Laws of Human Nature*, **Robert Greene**.

 The legendary business growth consultant and best-selling author of *The E-Myth* book series, **Michael Gerber**.

 The renowned business growth consultant and best-selling author of *The Traction* book series, **Gino Wickman**.

 Named to fast company's "100 Most Creative people in business" list, the co-creator of Behance, the Current VP of Products at Adobe, and best-selling author, **Scott Belsky**.

 Comedian and actress, **Rosanne Barr**.

 The actress, writer, producer, researcher, and podcast host, **Mel K**.

 The billionaire founder of Paychex, **Tom Golisano**.

 The Executive Vice President of the Trump Organization and son of America's 45th & 47th President, **Eric Trump**.

 The broadcaster, podcast host, influencer, and daughter-in-law of America's 45th & 47th President, **Lara Trump**.

 The American businessman, political activist, and son of America's 45th & 47th President, **Donald Trump Jr**.

 The best-selling author, entrepreneur and innovator in the fields of investing science and financial education, **Mark Manson**.

The author of seven *New York Times* bestsellers, former host and a co-executive producer of the National Geographic Channel social science TV series Crowd Control, and former speechwriter for Vice President, Al Gore, **Daniel Pink**.

 The blind best-selling author, movie producer, and entrepreneur, **Jim Stovall**.

 The owner and operator of multiple privately held companies, and a private equity real estate firm, Cardone Capital, with a multifamily portfolio of assets worth over $5 Billion. He is one of the Top Crowdfunders in the world, raising over $1.63 Billion in equity via social media, **Grant Cardone**.

 The iconic author, consultant, minister, and motivational speaker, **Eric Thomas**.

 The founding executive editor of Wired magazine and a former editor and publisher of the Whole Earth Review. He has also been a writer, photographer, conservationist, and student of Asian and digital culture, **Kevin Kelly**.

 The founder and former chairman and CEO of Gateway Mortgage Group and the Governor of Oklahoma, **Kevin Stitt**.

 Retired American military officer and politician who served as the 13th administrator of the National Aeronautics and Space Administration (NASA), **Jim Bridenstine**.

 A pioneer in the field of neurosurgery, retired neurosurgeon, academic, author, and government official who served as the 17th United States secretary of housing and urban development from 2017 to 2021, **Ben Carson**.

The lawyer who has served as the legal spokesperson for President Donald J. Trump, senior advisor for MAGA, Inc., Trump's Super PAC and the U.S. Attorney for the District of New Jersey, as well as Counselor to the President in the second Trump administration, **Alina Habba**.

 Prolific Top 40 Hit Song-Writer for Justin Bieber, Maroon 5, Gwen Stefani, Charlie Puth, Michael Buble, Jason Derulo, and James Taylor, **Ross Golan**.

 The director of the Federal Bureau of Investigation since 2025. He also served as acting director of the Bureau of Alcohol, Tobacco, Firearms, and Explosives from February to April 2025. After more than a dozen years in government service as a public defender, national security prosecutor, and JSOC civilian- he took senior leadership positions in the Trump Administration, including Chief of Staff for the Department of Defense (DoD), Deputy Director of National Intelligence, and Deputy Assistant to President Trump & Senior Director for Counterterrorism, **Kash Patel**.

 Best-selling author, co-founder and former President of the Ritz-Carlton, **Horst Schulze**.

 American professional basketball coach and former NBA player who held the position of point guard despite being under 6 feet tall. He currently is an assistant coach for the Boston Celtics of the National Basketball Association, **Phil Pressey**.

 American professional basketball coach and former NBA player who played for seven different NBA teams and is widely credited as being one of the first point forwards in the history of the NBA, **Paul Pressey**.

 The *New York Times* best-selling author of 40 million + books, journalist, and musician **Mitch Albom**.

The legendary MIT graduate and physicist who was brought on as a strategic consultant to work with James Cameron and Arnold Schwarzenegger on the creation of the SHOWTIME documentary called "YEARS OF LIVING DANGEROUSLY" starring Matt Damon, Jessica Alba, Don Cheadle, America Ferrera, Jack Black, Sigourney Weaver, Thomas Friedman, Olivia Munn, David Letterman, Gisele Bündchen, Joshua Jackson, and Harrison Ford. Rolling Stone has called him one of the "100 People Who Are Changing America", **Joseph Romm**.

 The former Director of Communications for Harley-Davidson Motor Company who successfully turned Harley-Davidson around as the company attempted to reemerge after filing for bankruptcy, **Ken Schmidt**.

 The legendary sports agent turned COO & Vice President of Team Sports for Wasserman. Wasserman represents Marshawn Lynch, Russell Westbrook, Mia Hamm, Draymond Green, Klay Thompson, etc. COO & Vice President of Team Sports. (**Jason Ranne**)

 The best-selling author and renowned Professor of Business Administration at the Harvard Business School who was regarded as one of the world's top experts on innovation and growth, **Clayton Christenson**.

 New York Times Best-Selling Author of Purple Cow, and former Yahoo! Vice President of Marketing, **Seth Godin**.

 A 5 foot 8 inch running back from Mulberry, Florida who became an NFL Pro Bowl running back. This former college teammate of Marshawn Lynch while playing college football at CAL has now turned into a successful entrepreneur, **Justin Forsett**.

 Commentator and Best-Selling Author, **Ben Shapiro**.

Co-Founder of the 700+ Employee Advertising Company (AdRoll), **Adam Berke**.

 Emmy Award-winning Producer of the Today Show and *New York Times* Best-Selling Author of *Sh*tty Moms*, **Mary Ann Zoellner**.

 International Best-Selling Author of *In Search of Excellence*, **Tom Peters**.

 NBA Player and Coach, **Muggsy Bogues** (Shortest player to ever play in the league).

 NFL Running Back and Winner of Dancing with the Stars, **Rashad Jennings**.

 The former Executive Vice President of Walt Disney World who once managed 40,000 employees, **Lee Cockerell**.

 Billboard Contemporary Christian Top 40 Recording Artist, **Colton Dixon**

 The founder of wikipedia, **Jimmy Wales**.

See additional guests at Thrivetimeshow.com

 If you are tired of being stuck in the rat-race and living amidst monetary mediocrity and career constipation, then this short, yet POWERFUL book is written for you. If you have been searching for the proven path to getting unstuck and to becoming financially free, then this unapologetically action-packed and fact-filled business-building book is for you.

NOTABLE QUOTABLE

"Knowledge has no value except that which can be gained from its application towards some worthy end."

- NAPOLEON HILL

(The best-selling author of Think & Grow Rich. Think & Grow Rich is the book that changed my life, thus I named my son Aubrey Napoleon-Hill Clark.)

When you begin working with a proven mentor, coaching program, consulting service or personal training service, you must decide that you are going to be coachable; because if you already knew the proven path and were diligently implementing a proven system, you wouldn't be stuck. Thus, moving forward, I am going to ASSUME that you have made the decision to be coachable, approachable, and willing to diligently implement what your PROVEN mentor, coaching program, consulting service or personal training service is going to teach you.

To encourage you that you have what it takes throughout the pages of this book, I am going to bombard you with a barrage of real-life business coaching client success stories for added MASSIVE ENCOURAGEMENT.

You can also find thousands of success stories in video form at www.ThrivetimeShow.com/testimonials.

NOTABLE QUOTABLE

"I want to encourage you to think about how you would actually feel if you were able to lose 10 pounds this year? How would you feel if you lost 40 pounds this year? What if this was the year that you were finally able to get unstuck with your fitness goals. Have you been looking for the secrets of achieving your fitness goals? What if the proven path to getting in the best shape of your life wasn't complicated, and it was 100% implementable? What if you could experience game-changing and life-giving results this year?! What if I told you that found within the pages of this book you could find the secret sauce that will allow you to achieve your fitness goals starting now?! Well for the next 45 days, I want you to read this book as though both your health and wealth depended upon it, BECAUSE IT DOES! It is my hope that this book and your diligence over the next 45 days will be the very thing that changes your life for the better!"

- COLTON CLAUSSEN

(The Founder of www.ClaussenTulsaPersonalTraining.com)

NOTABLE QUOTABLE

"Knowledge without application
is meaningless."

- NAPOLEON HILL

(The best-selling author of Think & Grow Rich. Think & Grow Rich is the book that changed my life, thus I named my son Aubrey Napoleon-Hill Clark, and I constantly spend my life telling the world about Napoleon-Hill.)

How Will a PROVEN Mentor, Coaching Program or Training Service Change Your Life?

Throughout the remaining pages of this action-packed business building success guide book, I am going to show you how a proven mentor will raise your expectations, show you the proven success equation, and dramatically increase your compensation- if you are willing to simply put in the work and follow a proven path.

NOTABLE QUOTABLE

"Start where you are, with what you have. Make something of it and never be satisfied."

- GEORGE WASHINGTON CARVER

(A man who was born into slavery and who became the legendary self-taught American botanist and inventor who actively promoted the alternative crops and methods that lead to the prevention of soil mineral depletion for African Americans. Before George Washington Carver, newly freed African Americans did not know how to raise crops that would not deplete their lands of vital nutrients and essential minerals.)

"The missing ingredient for nearly all of the 1,000-plus clients I have worked with directly to improve their businesses is pigheaded discipline and determination. We all get good ideas at seminars and from books, radio talk shows, and business-building gurus. The problem is that most companies do not know how to identify and adapt the best ideas to their businesses. Implementation, not ideas, is the key to real success."

– CHET HOLMES

(The late great legendary business consultant and best-selling author of The Ultimate Sales Machine. His nearly one thousand clients included major companies like Pacific Bell, NBC, Citibank, Warner Bros., GNC, Wells Fargo, Estee Lauder and Merrill Lynch.)

If you are ready to discover the practical plan to increase your expectations, learn the proven success equation and begin DRAMATICALLY increasing your compensation, read on!!!

Now without any further ado, let's raise those EXPECTATIONS. Every day that you and I have is a gift from God, and what we do with it is a gift to God and that includes RIGHT NOW. In fact, as I am writing this book to you and for you, I am stuck in an aluminum tube (plane) and thus, I get to decide what I will do with my time. As I look to my left, people are watching movies while wearing headphones provided by Delta Airlines. As I look to my right, people are watching movies while eating the snacks provided by Delta Airlines. As I look up a few aisles, I see more people watching more movies and more people watching more movies. A few people are scrolling through social media, but I am 100% confident that I am the only person on this plane writing a book. In fact, as I look around, I am 100% confident that only about 5% of the people on the plane or less are doing anything that is even remotely productive. But, I am choosing to write this book for your benefit. Why? Because I choose to view every minute of every day as a gift from God and what I do with it as a gift to God.

> "This is the day which the Lord hath made; we will
> rejoice and be glad in it."
>
> **- PSALM 118:24**
>
> *(A book written by King David, whom the Bible says was a man
> after God's own heart.)*

My friend, instead of mindlessly watching movies, why don't you and I get busy building a life that people would want to turn into a movie? I just cannot grasp why anyone would want to spend their day watching mindless movies and scrolling through social media. Decide right now that every day that you have is a gift from God and that what you do with EVERY second of every day is a gift to God. Decide right now to stop wasting your time on the following time-wasting activities and more:

Engaging In Gossip	Scrolling Through Social Media	Thinking About How to Solve Unsolvable Geopolitical Issues
Watching TV		

NOTABLE QUOTABLE

"Vision without execution is hallucination."

THOMAS EDISON

(The man who introduced the world to recorded audio, recorded video, the first practical lightbulb, GE, and countless other inventions and business concepts.)

FUN FACT:

Did You Know That the Average Person Now Spends 11.3 Hours Per Day Consuming Media According to Nielsen?

"American adults spend over 11 hours per day listening to, watching, reading or generally interacting with media."

https://www.nielsen.com/insights/2018/time-flies-us-adults-now-spend-nearly-half-a-day-interacting-with-media/

NOTABLE QUOTABLE

"He what walketh with wise men shall be wise: but a companion of fools shall be destroyed."

- PROVERBS 13:20

(From a controversial book known as the Bible.)

Ok, now that you have discovered how to free up 11.3 HOURS OF YOUR DAY, let's focus on firing flaky friends and getting rid of negative soul-sucking toxic relationships. Whether you hear it from me, you read it in the Bible, learn about it from Tim Ferriss or have it taught to you by Jim Rohn, the harsh reality is that you will ultimately become like the five people that you choose to spend the most time with. Because I grew up without money, I by default was around people without money and without a success mindset. When I built www.DJConnection. com into one of America's largest entertainment companies for weddings, I found myself constantly surrounded by rappers, potheads, club DJs, and people with copious amounts of personal problems. Why? Because I chose to become a disc jockey, and it turns out that most people that choose to become disc jockeys like to party, like to host parties, and like to hang around party people. Thus, I had to become very intentional about removing negative influences and people from my life-and yes, that included family. When you spend your nights and weekends helping your dysfunctional brother-in-law sort out his latest relationship crisis, or spend your time helping your business partners that refuse to pay their commissions and to honor their agreements, you are wasting the life God gave you, and are going to have a hard time finding time to turn your goals into reality.

NOTABLE QUOTABLE

"You are the average of the five people you
spend the most time with."

- JIM ROHN

(*The legendary self-help guru, best-selling author and mentor to Tony
Robbins. Jim Rohn mentored Mark R. Hughes (the founder of Herbalife
International) and life strategist Tony Robbins in the late 1970s. Others
who credit Rohn for influencing their careers include authors/lecturers
Mark Victor Hansen, Jack Canfield (Chicken Soup book series), Everton
Edwards (Hallmark Innovators Conglomerate), Brian Tracy, Darren
Hardy, Todd Smith, Kevin Garver, and T. Harv Eker. Rohn coauthored the
novel* Twelve Pillars *with Chris Widener.*)

When you choose to allow people that are constantly late
to ride with you to places, you will constantly be late. Remove
the negative friends, family, employees, and acquaintances
from your life, and you will find that your quality of life will
dramatically improve. Anytime you want an unproductive
and drama-filled experience, simply call these intentionally
dysfunctional people.

When you choose to allow people that smoke pot to be
around you, you will smell like marijuana at all times. Remove
the negative friends, family, employees, and acquaintances
from your life, and you will find that your quality of life will
dramatically improve and you won't smell like marijuana.

When you choose to spend your day surrounded by family members who are impregnating women to whom they are not married, this will bring drama into your life. Remove the negative friends, family, employees, and acquaintances from your life, and you will find that your quality of life will dramatically improve.

When you choose to allow people with drug problems into your daily life, this will bring productivity-killing drama into your life. Remove the negative friends, family, employees, and acquaintances from your life, and you will find that your quality of life will dramatically improve.

AN EPIC 50X CLAY CLARK CLIENT SUCCESS STORY.

"In October of 2016 we grossed $13K for the whole month, right now, it's 2018, the month of Oct, it's the 22nd, we've grossed $50K. So we really want to just thank you Clay and Vanessa for everything you've done. We love you guys...Clay really helped us with his systems, taking us to the point of having ten or more employees, or doubling our size, helped us double our incomes..."

- RYAN WIMPEY

(The founder of TipTopK9.com sharing about how Clay Clark helped them to transform their business.)

"I am Ryan Wimpey, I am originally from Tulsa, born and raised here. I definitely learned alot about life design and making sure that the business serves you. The linear workflow for us and getting everything out and documented on paper is really important. We have workflows that are kind of all over the place so having linear workflow and seeing that mapped out on multiple different boards is pretty awesome. That's pretty helpful for me. The atmosphere here is awesome. I definitely just stared at the walls figuring how to make my facility look like this place. This place rocks. It's invigorating, the walls are super...it's very cool. The atmosphere is cool. The people are nice. Very good learning atmosphere. I literally want to model it and steal everything that is here (at Clay Clark's office) at this facility and just create it just on our business side.

Clay is hilarious. I literally laughed so hard that I started having tears yesterday. The content is awesome off the charts! It's very interactive and you can raise your hand. The wizard teaches, but the wizard interacts and he takes questions and that is awesome. If you are not attending the conference you are missing three quarters to half of your life! You are missing the thought process. Just getting in the thought process of Clay Clark to me, just that is priceless. That's money!

There is no upsells or anything. The cost of this
conference is quite a bit cheaper than business college.
I went to a small private liberal arts college and got a
degree in business and I didn't learn anything like they
are teaching here. I didn't learn linear workflows, I
learned stuff that I'm not using and I haven't been using
for the last 9 years. So what they are teaching here is
actually way better than what I got at business school
and I went to what was actually ranked as a very good
business school. The information that you are going to
get is just VERY VERY beneficial and the mindset that you
are going to get."

- RYAN WIMPEY

*(The founder of TipTopK9.com sharing his experience attending
Clay Clark's 2-day interactive ThrivetimeShow.com business
conference.)*

When you choose to allow yourself to be around people
that constantly bring you urgent emotional situations that
need your direct involvement to solve the crisis, you will never
have time to build a proactive and successful life. Remove
the negative friends, family, employees, and acquaintances
from your life, and you will find that your quality of life will
dramatically improve.

When you choose to allow flaky family members to gossip
in your living room, you will find yourself always caught up
in the drama. Remove the negative friends, family, employees,
and acquaintances from your life, and you will find that your
quality of life will dramatically improve.

When your roommate constantly brings random sexual partners home, you are going to have a lot of drama in your life. Remove the negative friends, family, employees, and acquaintances from your life, and you will find that your quality of life will dramatically improve.

When you choose to allow employees in your office to date and then promote their love interests into positions of leadership within your company, you are going to have life problems. Remove the negative friends, family, employees, and acquaintances from your life, and you will find that your quality of life will dramatically improve.

When you choose to allow divisive and argumentative people to be around you, you will find that arguments and divisiveness is pervasive. Remove the negative friends, family, employees, and acquaintances from your life, and you will find that your quality of life will dramatically improve.

NOTABLE QUOTABLE

"The richest people in the world look for and build networks, everyone else looks for work."

- ROBERT KIYOSAKI

(Robert Kiyosaki is the legendary best-selling author of the Rich Dad Poor Dad book series, podcaster, real estate investor, entrepreneur and multi-time ThrivetimeShow.com Podcast guest. The Rich Dad Poor Dad series of books which has been translated into 51 languages and sold over 41 million copies worldwide.)

The more that you choose to intentionally surround yourself with successful people and proven coaches that know the way, show the way, and actually go the way that you want to go and grow in your life, you will find yourself succeeding at a much more rapid rate. My friend, this is your year! This is your year to raise your expectations, to learn the proven success equation, and to DRAMATICALLY increase your level of compensation. Let's raise those financial expectations NOW!

E.X.P.E.C.T.A.T.I.O.N.

E - Energy-Filled Focus

X - Excuse Killing

P - Priority Optimizing

E - Execution Focused

C - Change Agent

T - Time-Sensitive

A - Action Focused

T - Tracking Results

I - Iterating Until Perfection

O - On Time & On Mission

N - Never-Quit Mentality

NOTABLE QUOTABLE

"If you want to achieve massive success in any area
of your life, you must first become MASSIVELY
COMMITTED. Over the years, I have had the opportunity
to help many people to get into the best physical shape
of their lives. But in order for YOU to turn YOUR dreams
into reality, I need you to get committed for the next
45 days to simply showing up and following a proven
process. You aren't going to live long enough to learn
everything you need to know from scratch. When it
comes to fitness, I know the proven path, and I know
that you must take the first step today, and then you
must take the next step tomorrow. I can promise you
that if you will simply follow a proven workout routine
and a proven nutrition plan, you will achieve your fitness
goals this year!'

- COLTON CLAUSSEN

(The Founder of www.ClaussenTulsaPersonalTraining.com)

Throughout the Bible God Did Profound Things In 40 Day Increments? You Will Be Amazed At How Much Traction You Can Gain In Your Own Life Within 45 Days!

NOTABLE QUOTABLE

"Feeling stuck? Most entrepreneurs feel stuck because they have false expectations. Most entrepreneurs dramatically overestimate how much they can achieve in a week and underestimate the results they are capable of achieving within just one short year of diligently implementing proven plans and best-practice success systems."

- CLAY CLARK

(Oklahoma 2007 Young Small Business Administration Entrepreneur of the Year, best-selling author, ThrivetimeShow. com Podcast host, founder of several multi-million dollar businesses and co-founder of 5 children with one wonderful wife.)

FUN FACTS & BIBLICAL KNOWLEDGE:

* The number 40 appears in the Bible 159 times.

* The phrase "40 days and 40 nights" appears 24 times in the Bible.

* **Matthew 4:2** - Jesus was tempted by the devil for 40 days and 40 nights in the wilderness.

* **Genesis 7:7** - God told Noah that he would cause "it to rain upon the earth 40 days and 40 nights; and every living substance that I have made will I destroy from off the face of the earth."

* **Deuteronomy 8:2-5** - The Israelites wandered in the desert for 40 years.

* **Exodus 24:18** - Moses fasted for 40 days and 40 nights on Mount Sinai.

* **Genesis 7:12** - The rain for the Great Flood lasted for 40 days and 40 nights.

* **Numbers 13:25** - The Israelite spies took 40 days to explore the land of Canaan.

* **1 Samuel 17:16** - Goliath taunted the Israelite army for 40 days before David defeated him.

* **1 Kings 19:8** - Elijah traveled for 40 days and 40 nights to Mt. Horeb.

* **Ezekiel 4:6** - God instructed Ezekiel to bear the iniquity of the house of Judah for 40 days

* **Acts 1:3** - After His resurrection, Jesus appeared to his disciples over a period of 40 days.

* **2 Corinthians 11:24** - Paul mentions receiving 40 lashes from the Jews, minus one, on five separate occasions.

* **1 Samuel 17:16** - Goliath presented himself to Israel for 40 days.

* **Acts 13:21** - Saul reigned for 40 years

* **Numbers 13:25** - The spies searched the land of Canaan for 40 days

* **Judges 13:1** - Israel did evil; God gave them to an enemy for 40 years

* **1 Samuel 4:18** - Eli judged Israel for 40 years

* **Judges 12:14** - Abdon, a judge in Israel, had 40 sons

* **2 Samuel 2:10** - Ishbosheth (Saul's son) was 40 years old when he began to reign

* **2 Samuel 5:4 & 1 Kings 2:11** - David reigned over Israel for 40 years

* **1 Kings 11:42** - Solomon reigned the same length as his father, 40 years

* **1 Kings 6:17** - The holy place of the temple was 40 cubits long

* **1 Kings 19:8** - Elijah had one meal that gave him strength for 40 days

* **Ezekiel 4:6** - Ezekiel bore the iniquity of the house of Judah for 40 days

* **2 Kings 12:1** - Joash reigned 40 years in Jerusalem

* **Ezekiel 29:11-12** - Egypt to be laid desolate for 40 years

* **Jonah 3:4** - God gave Ninevah 40 days to repent.

* **Matthew 4:2** - Jesus fasted 40 days and nights.

* **Luke 4:2, Mark 1:13** - Jesus was tempted 40 days.

* **Acts 1:3** - Jesus remained on earth 40 days after the resurrection.

"[1] Then was Jesus led up of the Spirit into the wilderness to be tempted of the devil. [2] And when he had fasted FORTY days and FORTY nights, he was afterward an hungred. [3] And when the tempter came to him, he said, If thou be the Son of God, command that these stones be made bread. [4] But he answered and said, It is written, Man shall not live by bread alone, but by every word that proceedeth out of the mouth of God. [5] Then the devil taketh him up into the holy city, and setteth him on a pinnacle of the temple, [6] And saith unto him, If thou be the Son of God, cast thyself down: for it is written, He shall give his angels charge concerning thee: and in their hands they shall bear thee up, lest at any time thou dash thy foot against a stone. [7] Jesus said unto him, It is written again, Thou shalt not tempt the Lord thy God. [8] Again, the devil taketh him up into an exceeding high mountain, and sheweth him all the kingdoms of the world, and the glory of them; [9] And saith unto him, All these things will I give thee, if thou wilt fall down and worship me. [10] Then saith Jesus unto him, Get thee hence, Satan: for it is written, Thou shalt worship the Lord thy God, and him only shalt thou serve. [11] Then the devil leaveth him, and, behold, angels came and ministered unto him."

- MATTHEW 4:1-11

GOD CAN DO ALOT & YOU CAN DO ALOT IN JUST 40 DAYS

"¹ And the Lord said unto Noah, Come thou and all thy house into the ark; for thee have I seen righteous before me in this generation. ² Of every clean beast thou shalt take to thee by sevens, the male and his female: and of beasts that are not clean by two, the male and his female. ³ Of fowls also of the air by sevens, the male and the female; to keep seed alive upon the face of all the earth. ⁴ For yet seven days, and I will cause it to rain upon the earth FORTY days and FORTY nights; and every living substance that I have made will I destroy from off the face of the earth. ⁵ And Noah did according unto all that the Lord commanded him. ⁶ And Noah was six hundred years old when the flood of waters was upon the earth. ⁷ And Noah went in, and his sons, and his wife, and his sons' wives with him, into the ark, because of the waters of the flood. ⁸ Of clean beasts, and of beasts that are not clean, and of fowls, and of every thing that creepeth upon the earth, ⁹ There went in two and two unto Noah into the ark, the male and the female, as God had commanded Noah. ¹⁰ And it came to pass after seven days, that the waters of the flood were upon the earth. ¹¹ In the six hundredth year of Noah's life, in the second month, the seventeenth day of the month, the same day were all the fountains of the great deep broken up, and the windows of heaven were opened. ¹² And the rain was upon the earth FORTY days and FORTY nights."

- GENESIS 7:1-12

HOW MUCH CHANGE CAN YOU
MAKE IN JUST 45 DAYS?

"Becoming fully adapted to the Carnivore
Diet can require anywhere from 30 days to
perhaps 90 days for some people. The average
weight loss when individuals went on the 30-
Day Carnivore Diet is about 30 pounds...It's a
good idea to commit for at least that long in
your mind just to get started...Carnivore is a
big shift physically, but also psychologically.
Many people have come to view food as
entertainment, food is used as a soothing
mechanism to calm nerves, anxiety and
boredom...You do not need to count calories. In
fact you should aim to not be hungry. Meat is
one of the most satiating food things on earth.
Despite what you have heard you can survive
indefinitely on just beef as long as it has enough
fat in there. The protein in beef is outstanding...
Eat meat like it's your job in the beginning,
because it kind of is for awhile.

And then once you have kind of reached that point two months down the road or six months down the road where you change how you perceive nutrition...A lot of people find that even if they eat until they are completely full, they often lose weight which is kind of interesting. It's often very liberating. It's very freeing because they are not constantly thinking about food...That kind of goes away. It's kind of freedom from really an addiction."

- DOCTOR SHAWN BAKER

(The best-Selling author of Carnivore Diet, multiple-time Joe Rogan podcast guest, multiple-time ThrivetimeShow. com podcast guest and ThrivetimeShow.com Business Conference speaker.)

"Do you know that there is a big difference between an idle wish for the attainment of a definite object and a burning desire to attain it? Anybody can wish for things, and most people do, but only a few know how to desire so deeply that it turns into a flame of resolute determination."

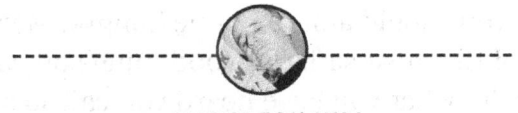

- NAPOLEON HILL

(The life-changing and best-selling author of Think & Grow Rich. Clay Clark named his son Aubrey Napoleon-Hill Clark after Napoleon Hill.)

"In the past many years I have analyzed 25,000 men and women in America. 98% of them are failures. And every failure has lacked a definite purpose in life. The 2% who succeed without exception, have a definite major aim in life, coupled with a burning desire to achieve it and for them success and wealth have followed as a night follows the day."

- NAPOLEON HILL

(Napoleon Hill is the best-selling author of the best-selling self-help book of all-time, Think & Grow Rich This book changed Clay Clark's life and thus Clay Clark named his son, Aubrey Napoleon-Hill Clark.)

"Inaction breeds doubt and fear. Action breeds confidence and courage. If you want to conquer fear, do not sit home and think about it. Go out and get busy."

- DALE CARNEGIE

(The legendary best-selling and self-help author of How to Win Friends & Influence People.)

"We know from observation and experience that the following principles, when assembled in the mind through a combination of thoughts, may produce mind power bordering upon the "miraculous":

a. Definiteness of Purpose

b. Self-Discipline, through control of the emotions

c. Controlled Attention

d. Imagination, applied to the object of one's purpose

e. Applied Faith, actively engaged"

- NAPOLEON HILL

(The life-changing and best-selling author of Think & Grow Rich. Clay Clark named his son Aubrey Napoleon-Hill Clark after Napoleon Hill.)

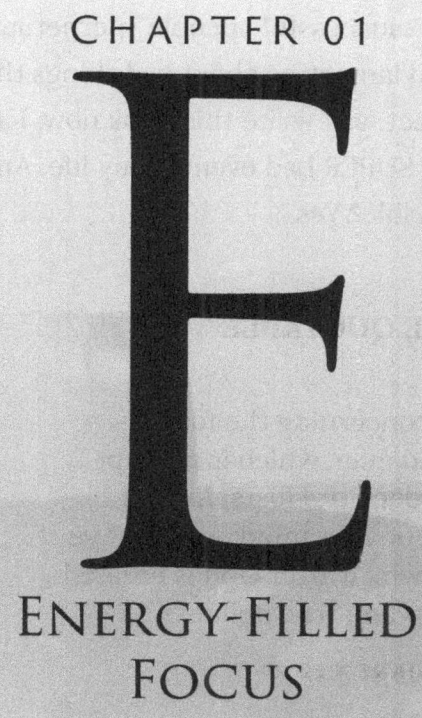

CHAPTER 01

E

ENERGY-FILLED
FOCUS

Over the years as I have intentionally sought out, paid for and prayed for mentorship from millionaires and billionaires, I have always been blown away at how consistently ENERGETIC super successful people are. In order to achieve massive success, a lot of energy is required, and I have found that ALL super successful people have sustained great and solution-focused energy. I have found that super successful people are very intentional about rebounding emotionally from setbacks and adversity quickly. A good mentor or coaching program is going to push you outside of your comfort zone and is going to encourage you and pressure you to bring more positive energy that you would typically bring to your work, your workout and to all that you do on a daily basis.

You won't find SUPER successful people perpetually yawning, moping around, and lamenting about bad things that have happened to them. In fact, as I write this book now, I am in the process of enduring a SUPER bad event in my life. Am I excited about it? No. Is it terrible? Yes.

NOTABLE QUOTABLE

"That ye put off concerning the former conversation the old man, which is corrupt according to the deceitful lusts; And be renewed in the spirit of your mind; And that ye put on the new man, which after God is created in righteousness and true holiness."

- EPHESIANS 4:22-24

> When my Dad died of Lou Gehrig's disease, did the world stop for me? No. Was it acceptable for me to stop making payroll, or to stop implementing my daily success systems and checklists? No.

> When my best friend died in a car accident, did this change the laws of success? No. Did the world stop to show me compassion? No.

> When I got sued for the first time, did the world of business change to accommodate me and my unique situation with compassion, kindness, and understanding? No.

> When my wife and I experienced a mis-carriage, did the pace of commerce slow down to accommodate our loss? No.

> When I had multiple top-level long-time employees
> start companies to compete directly with me by stealing
> systems, employees, and clients, did it stop me? No.

> When I was robbed multiple times, did the world stop and
> pity me? No. Did the average person lose sleep over it? No.

> When past employees have stolen equipment,
> money, clients, and systems, did America
> stop moving to see if I was ok? No.

> When I have had countless clients lie about the
> commission amounts owed to me which resulted in
> millions of dollars of lost commissions over the years,
> did capitalism stop to see if I was emotionally fine? No.

> Whenever I have had employees lie about the
> commission owed to them did God stop the
> events of the Earth to see if I was good? No.

> When I have had family members steal money from me
> did the economy take a timeout to check on me? No.

> When I have had family members impregnate other
> employees to whom they were not married to while
> working for me did the marketplace call a timeout
> to check on my emotional wellbeing? No.

> When I have had family members attempt to steal clients
> and employees from me did the state of Oklahoma
> declare a national emergency to help me recover? No.

> When every week, I am lied to by countless employees
> about their hours worked and why they can't
> work during their scheduled shifts does anyone
> ever check to see if I'm going to make it? No.

At some point, you and I must come to realize that nobody cares about your success more than you and I do. I really want you to be successful. However, you have to learn to kick your own tail in gear, to shut the hell up, and get back to work when bad things happen. When you are in business, bad things are going to happen, but you must choose to relentlessly bring great energy to your life and to your work every day. To make you feel less bad about your circumstances, I am going to make an EPIC list of terrible things that have happened to me over the past 29 years of self-employment which have not stopped me or reduced my enthusiasm for life and success at all.

"EVERY DAY, WAKE UP BEFORE EVERYONE
ELSE IN YOUR HOME DOES."

-CLAY CLARK

You and I should read Matthew 5:10-11 more often and know that it is true. You and I should read the book of Job more and know that it is true. You and I should read the book of Nehemiah more often and know that it is true. You and I should think about the millions of young children who die every year from a disease before they are even old enough to dream of achieving success. You and I must find a way to seize the day and turn all feelings of bitterness into feelings of betterness.

You and I cannot let horrible events slow us down or get in our way. We must continue to bring great energy all day. In order to maintain great energy, I choose to go to bed at 9:00 PM and wake up at 3:00 AM every day. I am not saying this is what you should do. However, I am saying that this is what I do. So what is my weekly schedule? I get up at 3 AM and I work until 6 PM, 6 days per week. Do you have to keep that schedule to become successful? No. I am just telling you that this is the schedule that I choose to keep. If you want to achieve massive success, you have to be willing to do what unsuccessful people are unwilling to do.

NOTABLE QUOTABLE

"Work like most people will not, so you can live like most people cannot."

- DAVE RAMSEY
(The legendary best-selling author, entrepreneur, radio talk show host, podcaster, financial guru, speaker and financial trainer.)

Bad Things Do Happen to Good People, And Bad Things Will Happen to You, But You Must Never Let This Lower the Amount of Energy That You Bring to Your Work and the Positivity That You Bring to Life.

I had one of my top disk jockeys (in the year 2000) decide to skip the wedding that he was scheduled to provide entertainment for so that he could fornicate (literally) with his dream woman. The bride was justifiably beyond upset, she demanded a refund (which I provided) and she would not let the issue go. The disk jockey who skipped the wedding had been a friend (I thought) of mine since college and felt absolutely zero remorse about the situation. While my young and growing company was suffering considerable financial harm, the response I was given was, "Hey, look man it's your business not mine." Yet, I did not let this situation drain my ENERGY or my focus. A good mentor will push you and hold you accountable to not letting events like this steal your ENERGY or your focus on the achievement of your goals.

Shortly after I had dealt with the sobering reality that I could not trust anyone and that one of my long-time friends would actually skip a wedding that he was scheduled to DJ for so that he could have sex with a woman, another bride took legal action against my company because she claimed that she was not happy with the level of entertainment that we provided. When I tried to reach the bride to discuss what happened and why she was unhappy with the service we provided, she would not take my calls and told me that she would only communicate with me via her attorney who wanted me to issue her a check for 5X what we originally charged her. At this point in my life I did not have good contracts in place to protect myself from legal action and so I quickly learned about the importance of having strong legal agreements in place. However, I did not let this situation drain my ENERGY or steal my focus. My friend, a good coach and trainer will push you and hold you accountable to not letting events like this steal YOUR ENERGY, YOUR DRIVE, or YOUR FOCUS on the achievement of your goals.

Over the years, nearly all of my top disk jockeys chose to violate their non-compete and non-solicitation agreements en route to starting their own disk jockey companies to compete directly with me. Yet, I did not let this situation drain my ENERGY or my focus. A good mentor will push you and hold you accountable to not letting events like this steal your ENERGY or your focus on the achievement of your goals.

Many of my top photographers chose to violate their non-compete and non-solicitation agreements to start competing companies by stealing my clients, my employees, and my systems.

Pictured left to right: Clay Clark (wearing the Minnesota Twins hat) with Mark DePetris (holding a birthday card). Mark DePetris was Clay Clark's best friend and a young man who was killed in a car accident while he was roommates in college with Clay Clark.

Pictured left to right: Clay Clark with Mark DePetris smoking cigars while roommates in college.

My best friend and life-long friend died in a car accident. Rest in Peace, Mark DePetris. Yet, I did not let this situation drain my ENERGY or my focus. A good mentor will push you and hold you accountable for not letting events like this steal your ENERGY or your focus on the achievement of your goals.

"The size of your success is measured by the strength of your desire; the size of your dream; and how you handle disappointment along the way."

- ROBERT KIYOSAKI

(Robert Kiyosaki is an international best-selling author of the Rich Dad Poor Dad book series, a legendary real estate investor, multiple-time ThrivetimeShow.com podcast guest, and entrepreneur. Kiyosaki is the author of more than 26 books, including the international self-published personal finance Rich Dad Poor Dad series of books which has been translated into 51 languages and sold over 41 million copies worldwide.)

Pictured left to right: Clay Clark and his father Thom Clark.

My father died of Lou Gherig's Disease (suffocation and body atrophy). Rest in Peace, Thom Clark (My Dad). Yet, I did not let this situation drain my ENERGY or my focus. A good mentor will push you and hold you accountable to not letting events like this steal your ENERGY or your focus on the achievement of your goals.

Many years ago a man came into my life seeking my business coaching and training. He explained to me that he was highly trained and skilled, and yet he could not afford to pay my regular monthly business coaching fee of $1,700 per month and he could not afford to rent an office space to run his business. He agreed to pay me a flat monthly coaching fee plus an agreed upon reasonable percentage of all sales moving forward. Over the nearly 8 years I worked with this man he let me know that he did not know how to find a team, build a team or train a team and that he needed my help. Then after 8 years of helping this man to scale a massive successful business he unapologetically let me know that he was simply no longer interested in honoring that agreement after it was discovered that he had been lying to me and had been aggressively shorting the monthly commission checks that he was supposed to pay to me. When I looked this man in the eye and asked him how he could do such a thing after I had helped him to go from poverty to prosperity, he simply told me that he no longer thought the deal was fair, but that I was welcome to talk to his attorney if I would like. However, I can sincerely tell you that I chose to not let this situation drain any of my ENERGY, FOCUS or MOMENTUM. My friend, a skilled coach and trainer will push you and hold you accountable for choosing not to let this type of personal and professional betrayal steal YOUR ENERGY, YOUR DRIVE, or YOUR FOCUS on the achievement of your goals.

" Develop success from failures.
Discouragement and failure are two of the
surest stepping stones to success."

- DALE CARNEGIE
(The legendary best-selling and self-help author of How to Win
Friends & Influence People.)

NOTABLE QUOTABLE

"People around you, constantly under the pull of their emotions, change their ideas by the day or by the hour, depending on their mood. You must never assume that what people say or do in a particular moment is a statement of their permanent desires."

- ROBERT GREENE, MASTERY

(A guest on the Thrive Time Show podcast, An iconic author on strategy and power. When reading Robert Greene's books it is important to know that people that do not read the Bible and who do not adhere to God's laws often use The 48 Laws of Power against you in a nefarious way. I believe that it's important to know the moves that nefarious people will use against you so that you can protect yourself against the evil moves and the problems they will cause you. He has written seven international bestsellers, including The 48 Laws of Power, The Art of Seduction, The 33 Strategies of War, The 50th Law (with rapper 50 Cent), Mastery, The Laws of Human Nature, and The Daily Laws.)

NOTABLE QUOTABLE

"Success consists of going from failure to
failure without loss of enthusiasm."

- WINSTON CHURCHILL

(Sir Winston Leonard Spencer Churchill (1874 – 1965) was a
British statesman, military officer, and writer who was Prime
Minister of the United Kingdom from 1940 to 1945 (during
the Second World War) and again from 1951 to 1955. Winston
Churchill chose to stand up alone against Adolf Hitler's quest to
take over Europe without the support of the United States. When
Winston Churchill stepped into the role of Prime Minister on
May 10, 1940 he decided to focus on increasing the resolve of the
British people who were on the verge of surrendering to the Nazi
regime as Britain faced the sobering reality of a Nazi invasion.
Churchill also worked tirelessly to convince the French to keep
fighting against the Nazis while simultaneously attempting to
convince President Franklin D. Roosevelt that he and his people
urgently needed the United States to fight against Adolph Hitler
and the Nazis if Great Britain was going to successfully defend
itself against the Nazi military powerhouse that was successfully
conquering near all of Europe.)

As an example of the unrelenting spirit and determination
of Winston Churchill this is an excerpt from the speech he
delivered to British Parliament on May 13th 1940 while choosing
to stand alone in his decision to not surrender or to reach a
compromise of any kind with Adolf Hitler and the Nazi Party.

"I say to the House as I said to ministers who have joined this government, I have nothing to offer but blood, toil, tears, and sweat. We have before us an ordeal of the most grievous kind. We have before us many, many months of struggle and suffering.

You ask, what is our policy? I say it is to wage war by land, sea, and air. War with all our might and with all the strength God has given us, and to wage war against a monstrous tyranny never surpassed in the dark and lamentable catalogue of human crime. That is our policy.

You ask, what is our aim? I can answer in one word. It is victory. Victory at all costs - Victory in spite of all terrors - Victory, however long and hard the road may be, for without victory there is no survival.

Let that be realized. No survival for the British Empire, no survival for all that the British Empire has stood for, no survival for the urge, the impulse of the ages, that mankind shall move forward toward his goal.

I take up my task in buoyancy and hope. I feel sure that our cause will not be suffered to fail among men. I feel entitled at this juncture, at this time, to claim the aid of all and to say, "Come then, let us go forward together with our united strength."

- Winston Churchilll

I had one of my top (and very tall) employees whom I had employed since he was 18 years old leave my company to work for a client of mine, while simultaneously attempting to recruit my entire staff to leave my team and to go work with him.

When you are pushing through adversity it is a rare trait to keep pushing to keep moving and to stay positive while relentlessly pursuing your goal without the loss of any enthusiasm.

NOTABLE QUOTABLE

"PERSISTENCE is an essential factor in the procedure of transmuting DESIRE into its monetary equivalent. The basis of persistence is the POWER OF WILL. Will-power and desire, when properly combined, make an irresistible pair. Men who accumulate great fortunes are generally known as cold-blooded, and sometimes ruthless. Often they are misunderstood. What they have is will-power, which they mix with persistence, and place back of their desires to insure the attainment of their objectives."

- NAPOLEON HILL
(The best-selling author of the book that changed my life, Think And Grow Rich. I would sincerely recommend that at some point YOU would read Think And Grow Rich because nothing is as powerful as a changed mind.)

Whatever adversity you are going through, I would encourage you to consider the examples listed below to encourage you to not stop and to not quit no matter how difficult the situation that you are facing.

AMPLE EXAMPLES OF SUCCESS GAINED THROUGH STRUGGLE

1. **Amazon** - Jeff Bezos and Amazon took 9 years to make a profit.

2. **Walt Disney** - Walt Disney lost it all twice.

3. **Tesla** - Tesla took over 10 years to make a profit (2003 - 2013)

4. **Thomas Edison** – Thomas Edison was expelled from school, and developed countless failed experiments. However, Thomas Edison and his team created 10,000 failed experiments before creating and inventing the first functional and practical light bulb. Thomas went on to invent recorded audio, recorded video and to found one of the most successful companies in American history (General Electric). Thomas Edison went on to gain 1,093 U.S. patents for his inventions.

5. **Henry Ford** - Henry Ford financially lost it all 5 times.

6. **FedEx** – Frederick W. Smith, and his company FedEX did not make a profit for 10 years.

7. **Facebook** – Mark Zuckerberg and Facebook lost over $3 million during their first 3 years.

8. **Google** - Larry Page and Sergey Brin originally founded Google under the name."Backrub" which did not make a profit from 1996 to 1999.

9. **ESPN** - Bill Rasmussen, his son Scott Rasmussen and Ed

Egan launched ESPN in 1978 and did not make a profit until 1985.

10. **Dyson Vacuum** - It took James Dyson 15 years and 5,127 attempts to create his first functional bagless cyclonic vacuum that entered into the actual marketplace.

11. **Ziploc** - It took the inventors of the Ziplock bag 17 years to crack the marketplace.

12. **President Abraham Lincoln** - Abraham Lincoln experienced losses and setbacks in nearly every imaginable way before becoming President of the United States. Abraham failed in business in 1833. Abraham's girlfriend died in 1835. Abraham had a nervous breakdown in 1836. Abraham was defeated for nomination in Congress in 1843. Abraham was rejected for land officer in 1849. Abraham was defeated in his attempt to join the U.S. Senate in 1854. Abraham was defeated for nomination for Vice President in 1856. Abraham was defeated again in his attempt to join the U.S. Senate in 1858. Abraham was elected President of the United States in 1860 and faced nearly total opposition from everyone when it came to his belief that the practice of slavery should be abolished in this country that we now call the United States of America.

13. **Steve Jobs** was actually fired from the company he started (Apple) after multiple product failures. However,

he returned to lead Apple to become one of the most successful companies on the planet.

As an entrepreneur who has successfully coached thousands of entrepreneurs across the finish line and to the achievement of success, I will tell you that procrastination and lack of persistence of this MASSIVE OBSTACLE facing most people most of the time. Remember, inaction is your giant, action is your sword and inspiration is your reward.

Napoleon Hill obsessively wrote about the importance of persistence including the following life-changing passage from his life-changing book, *Think And Grow Rich*.

NOTABLE QUOTABLE

"SYMPTOMS OF LACK OF PERSISTENCE

Here you will find the real enemies which stand between you and noteworthy achievement. Here you will find not only the "symptoms" indicating weakness of PERSISTENCE, but also the deeply seated subconscious causes of this weakness. Study the list carefully, and face yourself squarely IF YOU REALLY WISH TO KNOW WHO YOU ARE, AND WHAT YOU ARE CAPABLE OF DOING. These are the weaknesses which must be mastered by all who accumulate riches.

Failure to recognize and to clearly define exactly what one wants.

Procrastination, with or without cause. (Usually backed up with a formidable array of alibis and excuses).

Lack of interest in acquiring specialized knowledge.

Indecision, the habit of "passing the buck" on all occasions, instead of facing issues squarely. (Also backed by alibis.)

The habit of relying upon alibis instead of creating definite plans for the solution of problems.

Self-satisfaction. There is but little remedy for this affliction, and no hope for those who suffer from it.

Indifference, usually reflected in one's readiness to compromise on all occasions, rather than meet opposition and fight it.

The habit of blaming others for one's mistakes, and accepting unfavorable circumstances as being unavoidable.

WEAKNESS OF DESIRE, due to neglect in the choice of MOTIVES that impel action.

Willingness, even eagerness, to quit at the first sign of defeat. (Based upon one or more of the 6 basic fears).

Lack of ORGANIZED PLANS, placed in writing where they may be analyzed.

The habit of neglecting to move on ideas, or to grasp opportunity when it presents itself.

WISHING instead of WILLING.

The habit of compromising with POVERTY instead of aiming at riches. General absence of ambition to be, to do, and to own.

Searching for all the short-cuts to riches, trying to GET without GIVING a fair equivalent, usually reflected in the habit of gambling, endeavoring to drive "sharp" bargains.

FEAR OF CRITICISM, failure to create plans and to put them into action, because of what other people will think, do, or say. This enemy belongs at the head of the list, because it generally exists in one's subconscious mind, where its presence is not recognized."

- NAPOLEON HILL

(The best-selling author of the book that changed my life, Think And Grow Rich. I would sincerely recommend that at some point YOU would read Think And Grow Rich because nothing is as powerful as a changed mind.)

"We have been a client of Clay Clark for just over a year and a half. In the first year Clay Clark helped us grow by 96%. In this past year Clay Clark helped us to grow an additional 67%. I can't say enough about Clay Clark and his team. They are absolutely amazing. He is very proactive and very intuitive. He anticipates problems and has helped us set up processes and systems to deal with those problems before they even arise. It has been an overall great experience. We are thankful that he works with us. I just can't thank him enough for all of the work that he has done for our company."

- LEAH CALVERT

(Founder of the screen printing, embroidery and laser engraving company, 918DesignCompany.com)

A long-time client and business partner of mine decided to stop honoring their signed agreement with me, despite the fact that I helped them to grow their business by 65X, simply because they wanted to keep more of the money for themselves. Yet, I did not let this situation drain my ENERGY or my focus. A good mentor will push you and hold you accountable to not letting events like this steal your ENERGY or your focus on the achievement of your goals.

I had a business partner simply decide to stop honoring our signed partnership agreement, after we had helped him to grow his business by over 20X, simply because she wanted to keep more money for herself. When they relentlessly tried to hire my entire staff away from me, I did not let this steal my joy, my energy, or my focus. A good mentor will push you and hold you accountable to not letting events like this steal your ENERGY or your focus on the achievement of your goals.

The lockdowns, quarantines, and mandates related to COVID-19 killed many businesses all around the world. Yet, did I let this situation drain my ENERGY or my focus? NO!!! A good mentor will push you and hold you accountable to not letting events like this steal your ENERGY or your focus on the achievement of your goals.

"Clay, you are an entrepreneur and I'm an entrepreneur. Clay it's my honor to be on your show and thank you for all you do. I hear the ripple effects from you are good ripple effects. People rave about what they learn from you so congratulations!"

- ROBERT KIYOSAKI

(Robert Kiyosaki is an international best-selling author of the Rich Dad Poor Dad book series, a legendary real estate investor, multiple-time ThrivetimeShow.com podcast guest, and entrepreneur. Kiyosaki is the author of more than 26 books, including the international self-published personal finance Rich Dad Poor Dad series of books which has been translated into 51 languages and sold over 41 million copies worldwide.)

"You certainly were the on-site leader that we needed for this calling campaign. By watching you work with these students and seeing the result, I became reassured that hiring you to do exactly what you did was the right thing to do. Your team brought in over $120K in gifts and pledges, which may be an all-time ORU phonathon record! But I'll have more for you later. Again, thanks for everything....and don't drink too much Red Bull!"

- JESSE D. PISORS

(B.A. (1996) M.A. (2005) | Director of Alumni & Ministerial Relations and Annual Fund | www.ORU.edu)

NOTABLE QUOTABLE

"As a Tulsa personal trainer, my job is to help get my clients into the best shape of their lives. In order to do that, I must be a source of inspiration and motivation for my clients. I try not to be a source of irritation for my clients, but if that has to happen in order to provoke positive change, sometimes this must happen. But I can tell you that nothing will change unless I bring the energy to each personal training session, and unless my client is willing to put in the effort and energy as well. As a fitness mentor, I have found that the energy I bring each and every day to my personal training sessions is contagious, and that is what clients pay me for. If you need inspiration from an outside source, you are not alone. Most people need a proven mentor, a coach or some type of personal trainer or group fitness class to keep them engaged and motivated to do what needs to be done in the area of fitness."

- COLTON CLAUSSEN

(The Founder of www.ClaussenTulsaPersonalTraining.com)

NOTABLE QUOTABLES

"Blessed are they which are persecuted for righteousness' sake: for theirs is the kingdom of heaven."

- MATTHEW 5:10

"For the love of money is the root of all evil:
which while some coveted after, they have
erred from the faith, and pierced themselves
through with many sorrows."

1 TIMOTHY 6:10

FUN FACT:

"Litigation . . . impossible to plan for, but inevitable for most businesses. Statistics show...90% of all businesses are engaged in litigation at any given time...that somewhere between 36%-53% of small businesses are involved in at least one litigation in any given year."

https://www.forbes.com/sites/basharubin/2014/07/14/youre-going-to-get-sued/

If you are in business, you are going to get screwed and be sued. I would encourage you to remember that God is always watching and to always do the right thing even when no other humans are watching. Remember that the Bible states in Proverbs 1:7- "The fear of the Lord is the beginning of knowledge: but fools despise wisdom and correction." It is going to happen. You can't control what happens to you. You can control how you choose to respond to the things that happen to you. My friend, when you choose to team up with a proven mentor or coaching program, they will help you navigate the horrible, terrible, bad, and negative things that are going to happen to you. However, the best way to avoid criticism, push back, and negativity is to simply do nothing.

NOTABLE QUOTABLE

"Criticism is something you can easily avoid
— by saying nothing, doing nothing, and
being nothing."

- ARISTOTLE

(Aristotle was an Ancient Greek philosopher and polymath. His writings cover a broad range of subjects spanning the natural sciences, philosophy, linguistics, economics, politics, psychology, and the arts.)

NOTABLE QUOTABLE

"You have enemies? Good. That means you've
stood up for something, sometime in your life."

- WINSTON CHURCHILL

(Sir Winston Leonard Spencer Churchill was a British statesman, military officer, and writer who was Prime Minister of the United Kingdom from 1940 to 1945 (during the Second World War) and again from 1951 to 1955. He was the sole leader in Europe to stand up to and against the genocidal and world takeover plans of Adolph Hitler and The Nazi party.)

FUN FACT

"75% of employees have stolen from their employer at least once, according to the U.S. Chamber of Commerce. The Chamber also found that up to 30% of business failures may be the result of employee fraud and abuse"

Your Employees Are Probably Stealing From You. Here Are Five Ways To Put An End To It. - https://www.forbes.com/sites/ivywalker/2018/12/28/your-employees-are-probably-stealing-from-you-here-are-five-ways-to-put-an-end-to-it/

When you have a proven mentor or coach in your life pushing you with increased energy and momentum you are simply able to run right over the adversity that would typically slow many entrepreneurs down.

As an example, we helped a client by the name of www. GiveADerm.com to grow their skincare business by 4,000% within 1 year. How did we do this? Well, when I first met the founders of www.GiveADerm.com, I immediately picked up on their passion for their product and their mission of creating healthy skin care products. However, your business, their business and every business will quickly go to hell if you can't sell. That is where they needed help.

They needed to get their products in front of their ideal and likely buyers IMMEDIATELY, and in order to do this we needed to infuse BIG OVERWHELMING OPTIMISTIC MOMENTUM and CONTAGIOUS ENERGY into their businesses. We needed to help them to reach out to as many solid social media influencers as possible within a short period of time.

> Was there a massive amount of rejection we faced when marketing to social media influencers? Yes.

> Were there many big-time rejections from big-time influencers? Yes.

> Did the rejections feel good? No.

> However, I worked with the founders, Juliana & Deborah to help them learn how to turn bitterness into betterness and how to turn the hateful rejections into the figurative HATERADE beverage needed to fuel their fire of desire.

> Did I take copious amounts of time to lament over every rejection? No.

> Did I invest massive amounts of time discussing their feelings of rejection and my feelings of rejection? No.

I focused the www.GiveADerm.com team on taking MASSIVE ACTION, which creates MASSIVE AMOUNTS OF REJECTION and MASSIVE MOMENTUM!!! My friend, you must bring positive energy to every aspect of your business and the process of improving your life or you will lose.

A proven mentor and coaching program will encourage you to grow through whatever adversity you are experiencing without allowing you to lose momentum and to become a sorrowful, slothful, slow-moving, and fearful sack of mediocrity. Even as I am writing these words right now, I was just informed that an employee was making unwanted sexual advances at another employee for a business that I'm involved in. This morning, another employee for a company I work with has now decided to switch their gender and has demanded that we address them based upon their new gender. Meanwhile, I'm just trying to write a book and help you to achieve your goals. As entrepreneurs, the adversity never stops. Did I mention I also just discovered the internet is not working properly at one of my grooming lounges?

If you want to achieve success you must develop the power of persistence. You must learn how to turn rejection into your source of inspiration upon further inspection. You must learn how to transform irritation into motivation. You must learn how to become inspired to do what is required. You must insist on developing a persistent attitude and having self-discipline if you want to win. My friend if you want to achieve massive success in life you must learn how to turn the power of persistence into your SUPER POWER! Read the following NOTABLE QUOTABLE below from Napoleon Hill's *Think And Grow Rich*, to discover the proven formula for developing persistence.

NOTABLE QUOTABLE

"Later in life, after having analyzed thousands of people, I discovered that MOST IDEAS ARE STILLBORN, AND NEED THE BREATH OF LIFE INJECTED INTO THEM THROUGH DEFINITE PLANS OF IMMEDIATE ACTION. The time to nurse an idea is at the time of its birth. Every minute it lives, gives it a better chance of surviving. The FEAR OF CRITICISM is at the bottom of the destruction of most ideas which never reach the PLANNING and ACTION stage. How TO DEVELOP PERSISTENCE

There are four simple steps which lead to the habit of PERSISTENCE. They call for no great amount of intelligence, no particular amount of education, and but little time or effort. The necessary steps are:

A DEFINITE PURPOSE BACKED BY BURNING DESIRE FOR ITS FULFILLMENT.

A DEFINITE PLAN, EXPRESSED IN CONTINUOUS ACTION.

A MIND CLOSED TIGHTLY AGAINST ALL NEGATIVE AND DISCOURAGING INFLUENCES, including negative suggestions of relatives, friends and acquaintances.

A FRIENDLY ALLIANCE WITH ONE OR MORE PERSONS WHO WILL ENCOURAGE ONE TO FOLLOW THROUGH WITH BOTH PLAN AND PURPOSE.

These four steps are essential for success in all walks of life. The entire purpose of the thirteen principles of this philosophy is to enable one to take these four steps as a matter of habit.

These are the steps by which one may control one's economic destiny.

They are the steps that lead to freedom and
independence of thought.

They are the steps that lead to riches, in small or
great quantities.

They lead the way to power, fame, and
worldly recognition.

They are the four steps which guarantee
favorable "breaks."

They are the steps that convert dreams into
physical realities."

- NAPOLEON HILL

*(The best-selling author of the book that changed my life, Think
And Grow Rich. I would sincerely recommend that at some point
YOU would read Think And Grow Rich because nothing is as
powerful as a changed mind.)*

"I had the pleasure of working with Mr. Clark in 2010 when I managed over 2.2 million square feet of downtown office and retail space. I can recommend him highly and without reservation. I had hired Mr. Clark to rebrand the portfolio, and to reach out to prospective tenants. Throughout the course of the campaign, Mr. Clark was a consummate professional. He conducted market research, built a web-site, and coordinated obtaining pictures, print materials, and gaining media attention with-in what I would deem record time. With-in the first week of Mr. Clark going public with the campaign, he generated hundreds of prospective tenants. Mr. Clark's positive attitude is contagious, he is a hard worker, and he is genuinely a great guy to work with. I hope that in the near future I will have the opportunity to work with Mr. Clark again."

- DAVID ATKINSON | ONE PLACE, LLC | 120 W. 3RD STREET, TULSA, OK 74103

"The attendees all left with pages and pages of takeaways. They really enjoyed the energy, and the SPECIFIC ACTION POINTS you gave everybody. You and our Accounting Presenter got top marks. You really made this year's training EPIC."

- ANITRA NICHOLS | MAYTAG UNIVERSITY

CHAPTER 02

X

EXCUSE
KILLING

If you have a brain that is functioning well enough to read this book, then you too can make up, dream up, and develop excuses for sleeping in, slacking, drifting, not following a proven path, and melting into the mediocre mindset embraced by the masses. If just .00108% of the population is successful by default, why do Doctor Zoellner and I just keep winning over and over again? We don't make excuses for not implementing the proven principles and best-practice success systems that have been proven to work. After having worked with thousands of clients to help them to achieve massive success, I can tell you the patterns I see—NEARLY ALL OF THE CLIENTS that I have helped to build SUPER SUCCESSFUL businesses choose to develop the following habits-

> **SUCCESS HABIT #1**
>
> They all work off of a to-do list that they use to organize their day and follow up on action items over and over again until the successful completion of each action item.

> **SUCCESS HABIT #2**
>
> They all choose to use a calendar to organize their day and to organize their life. They choose to know where they are supposed to be and when they are supposed to be. ALL OF THE SUCCESSFUL clients that I have ever worked with understand that without a calendar in place, your day will drift.

> **SUCCESS HABIT #3**
>
> They rarely make excuses for not getting an action item done. If my successful clients say they are going to write 1,000 words of original content for each page of their website by Monday, they get it done. If my successful clients say they are going to be attending our weekly coaching meeting at our mutually agreed time, 95 times out of 100 they are ready to go on-time and on-mission. Successful people have developed the habit of not making excuses in a world where most people make excuses for most things most of the time.

NOTABLE QUOTABLE

"Unless commitment is made, there are only promises
and hopes... but no plans."

- PETER DRUCKER

*(The legendary management expert and author of 39 books
whose work helped revolutionize industry and to dramatically
increase the productivity in many large corporations and
industries, including the automotive industry.)*

Over the decades, I have often heard people tell me at conferences that they want to have success, but...

They are too old to become successful.

They are too young to become successful.

They forgot what they needed to do to become successful.

They don't have enough money to become successful.

They don't have enough connections to become successful.

They don't have enough time to become successful.

They are overwhelmed and don't even know where to start to become successful.

They are a big picture person and they don't have the mental capacity to focus long enough to become successful.

They believe their industry is different and thus they can't just follow a proven plan to become successful.

They are married to a spouse who doesn't share their vision enough to become successful.

They are not an early morning person and thus they don't have the time to become successful.

They aren't good enough at managing people to accomplish their action items.

They have lost the motivation to become successful.

They live in the wrong part of the country to be successful.

They have the wrong college degree to become successful.

"ACTION IS THE REAL MEASURE OF INTELLIGENCE."
– NAPOLEON HILL

However, a proven mentor or coaching program is going to encourage you to shut the hell up and get back to the work of moving towards the achievement of your goals. A proven mentor and coaching program is going to push you to be your best and stop believing your own excuses. A solid coach is going to be comfortable with making you get out of your comfort zone and the perpetual poverty zone of mindless mediocrity that will keep you poor.

NOTABLE QUOTABLE

"It doesn't matter if you come from the inner city. People who fail in life are people who find lots of excuses. It's never too late for a person to recognize that they have potential in themselves."

- BEN CARSON

(A ThrivetimeShow.com Podcast guest, an American retired neurosurgeon, academic, author, and government official who served as the 17th United States secretary of housing and urban development from 2017 to 2021. A pioneer in the field of neurosurgery, he was a candidate for President of the United States in the 2016 Republican primaries. Carson is one of the most prominent black conservatives in the United States.)

NOTABLE QUOTABLE

"Ninety-nine percent of the failures come from people who have the habit of making excuses."

- GEORGE WASHINGTON CARVER

(A man who was born a slave, yet went on to become an agricultural scientist and inventor who promoted alternative crops to cotton and methods to prevent soil depletion. He was one of the most prominent black scientists of the early 20th century.)

NOTABLE QUOTABLE

The way to get started is to quit talking and begin doing."

- WALT DISNEY

(Walt began developing his skills as a cartoonist as a very young kid while living on a farm in Missouri. Walt did the voice for Mickey Mouse. Walt Disney won 22 Academy Awards and was nominated for an Academy Award 59 times. If you do your research, it could be argued that it took Walt Disney 4,015 nights to become an overnight success story.)

If you have found yourself becoming very good at making excuses and justifications for not getting things done and for not demanding excellence from yourself on a daily basis, then you need a proven mentor or coaching program to push and pull you to success. Pro athletes have coaches. Professional actors, speakers and business leaders have coaches to teach them the proven systems and methodologies to hold them accountable and to help them measure their improvement.

NOTABLE QUOTABLE

"Professionals hire coaches and amateurs do not."

- ROBERT KIYOSAKI

(The legendary author of The Rich Dad Poor Dad book series, the successful investor, iconic podcaster, prolific educator and multiple time www.ThrivetimeShow.com Podcast guest.)

If you want to become a SUPER SUCCESSFUL entrepreneur, you must learn how to eliminate all excuses and all distractions that are standing in the way of you achieving your goal. In the classic self-help book, *Think & Grow Rich*, that changed my life, Napoleon Hill describes the potential power that can be generated when you resolve in your mind to have an unwavering commitment to the achievement of your goal after you have decided to eliminate the options of retreat when it comes to achieving success:

NOTABLE QUOTABLE

"A long while ago, a great warrior had to make a decision
which ensured his success on the battlefield. He was
about to send his armies against a powerful foe, whose
men outnumbered his own. He loaded his soldiers into
boats, sailed to the enemy's country, unloaded soldiers
and equipment, then gave the order to burn the ships
that had carried them. Addressing his men before
the first battle, he said, 'You see the boats going up in
smoke. That means that we cannot leave these shores
alive unless we win! We now have no choice - we win
or we perish!' They won. Every person who wins in any
undertaking must be willing to burn his ships and cut all
sources of retreat. Only by doing so can one be sure of
maintaining that state of mind known as a burning desire
which is to win, essential to success."

- NAPOLEON HILL

*(The legendary best-selling author of Think & Grow Rich. This
book, Think and Grow Rich, forever changed my mindset when
it comes to achieving success, over-delivering, who I choose to
surround myself with, the environment I allow myself to work in,
and more.)*

To become successful, your branding must be first class, your marketing must be effective, your sales systems must be fully developed, your team must be held accountable, and your product must WOW your ideal and likely buyers by solving their problems in a scalable and profitable way. The marketplace does not care about our excuses. The marketplace demands results; the market can fire you and everybody else that works with you by simply choosing to not spend their money with you and I.

NOTABLE QUOTABLE

"I tell everybody the same thing: You have to make every dish so when you taste it, you should remember it when you go home."

- WOLFGANG PUCK

(A *www.ThrivetimeShow.com* Podcast guest, the legendary *Chef, investor, restauranteur, entrepreneur and world-wide culinary icon.*)

As entrepreneurs, we need somebody that is 100% focused on giving us honest, objective, and constructive criticism on behalf of our future success, our wallets and our families. We need someone to point out that our website is not looking the best, that our workflow needs improvement, that our quality is slacking and we can take specific actions to improve our business, or that our quality can go to the next level.

NOTABLE QUOTABLE

"The Tiffany Theory states that a gift delivered in a box from Tiffany's will have a higher perceived value than one in no box or a plain box. That's not because the recipient is a fool; it's because in our society, we gift-wrap everything: our politicians, our corporate heads, our movie and TV stars, and even our toilet paper. Public Relations is like gift wrapping."

- MICHAEL LEVINE

(Thrive15.com mentor, multiple-time www.ThrivetimeShow. com Podcast Guest, best selling author and the PR consultant of choice for Michael Jackson, Pizza Hut, Nike, Prince, etc.)

If you want to grow a successful business, you must work tirelessly to implement the success strategies that have been proven to work. As an example, I had the opportunity to work with a super kind and hard-working entrepreneur and home remodeler by the name of Ronnie Morales. Ronnie is the founder of www.MoralesBrothers.net, which is based in Rosenberg, Texas. Ronnie had been listening to our shows for over 5 years, when he finally decided to attend one of our in-person workshops in Tulsa, Oklahoma. After just a year in our one-on-one business coaching program, we were able to help Ronnie grow his home remodeling business by 57%. How did we help Ronnie to grow his business by 57% in just one year? I showed Ronnie the proven plan and both he and I agreed that we would work the plan together, with no excuses.

When I showed Ronnie that he needed to write 1,000 words of original (HTML / hypertext markup language) content per page of his website. He knocked it out.

When I showed Ronnie that he needed to film an "About Us" video for his website to clearly communicate his ideal and likely buyers of his unique value proposition, Ronnie got it done.

When I showed Ronnie that he needed to gather objective testimonials and reviews from his real customers, he did the job.

Ronnie, didn't make excuses. Ronnie wanted to take his business to the next level and he knew that he didn't have time for excuses. Growing a business by 57% in just one year is remarkable, not-normal and certainly mind-blowing to most long-time business owners, but Ronnie did it because he didn't make excuses. As a business coach, my focus is on the following:

 Showing and teaching entrepreneurs the proven path.

 Helping entrepreneurs to implement the proven path.

 Holding entrepreneurs accountable to getting the work done.

 Tracking the results.

 Scaling the systems and processes that will ultimately allow a business to grow exponentially.

However, nothing will work unless you do. If you want to grow a successful business, you must diligently implement the proven best-practice business plan below. You don't have time for excuses, which is why ALL SUPER SUCCESSFUL ENTREPRENEURS that I have EVER interviewed have a proven mentor or coaching program in their corner pushing them, cheering for them, teaching them the proven systems, and holding them accountable for diligently implementing the proven processes and success systems that will only work if you put in the work.

> Step 1 - Establish Your Revenue Goals

> Step 2 - Determine Your Break-Even Numbers

> Step 3 - Define the Number of Hours Per Week You Are Willing to Work

> Step 4 - Define Your Unique Value Proposition

> Step 5 - Improve Branding

> Step 6 - Create 3-Legged Marketing Stool & a Powerful No-Brainer

> Step 7 - Create a Sales Conversion System

> Step 8 - Determine Sustainable Customer Acquisition Costs

> Step 9 - Create Repeatable Systems, Processes & File Organization

> Step 10 - Create Management Execution Systems

> Step 11 - Create a Sustainable & Repetitive Weekly Schedule

> Step 12 - Create Human Resources & Recruitment Systems

> Step 13 - Create Accounting & Automate Earning Millions

> Step 14 - Determine the Point of Achieving Financial Success

NOTABLE QUOTABLE

"Discipline is the bridge between goals and accomplishment."

- JIM ROHN

(The legendary self-help guru, best-selling author and mentor to Tony Robbins. Jim Rohn mentored Mark R. Hughes (the founder of Herbalife International) and life strategist Tony Robbins in the late 1970s. Others who credit Rohn for influencing their careers include authors/lecturers Mark Victor Hansen and Jack Canfield (Chicken Soup book series), Everton Edwards (Hallmark Innovators Conglomerate), Brian Tracy, Darren Hardy, Todd Smith, Kevin Garver, T. Harv Eker. Rohn coauthored the novel Twelve Pillars with Chris Widener.)

"I have the opportunity to train and work with many smart fitness clients and I have found that the smarter we are, the better we become at making excuses. Bottom line, either our fitness is a priority or it is not. I encourage you to stop the excuses and to begin scheduling time into your calendar for fitness and the achievement of your fitness goals. You must remember that what gets scheduled gets done."

- COLTON CLAUSSEN

(The founder of www.ClaussenTulsaPersonalTraining.com)

REDEEM THIS PAGE

COLTON CLAUSSEN

—TO GET—

ONE FREE WEEK

OF

PERSONAL TRAINING

$400 VALUE

Schedule Your First Free Week of Life-Changing Personal Training at ClaussenTulsaPersonalTraining.com

"I believe that the secret of your success is determined by your daily agenda. If you make a few key decisions and then manage them well in your daily agenda, you will succeed. Get control of your calendar; otherwise other people will."

- JOHN MAXWELL

(John Maxwell has been a multiple time guest on the ThrivetimeShow.com Podcast and is known as a legendary leadership expert and multiple-time New York Times best-selling author who has sold over 20 million copies of his books. Throughout John Maxwell's career, he has served as a senior pastor of multiple churches and he has been the keynote speaker of choice for The United States Military Academy at West Point, the National Football League, Keller Williams, Delta Airlines, Microsoft and countless Fortune 500 companies.)

"We have grown 3X. Working with Clay Clark has been a journey that really took the lid off of me or I would be in crisis right now. I would be 65 and would still have to be twisting wrenches right now and would be in that mode I was in when I first came to Clay Clark. I didn't have systems and processes. I can now take a week or two off without getting a call. If you knew what you needed to change in your business you would have already changed it. If you want to change you need to change. I would encourage everybody, even for your health and your marriage to fix your business, you need to fix your business."

- ROY COGGESHALL

(The founder of RCAutoSpecialists.com, TheGarageBA.com and TulsaTruckaccessoriesstore.com)

"I came out to Clay Clark's conference years ago and that is how I got introduced to ThrivetimeShow.com. We have seen our recurring services go up by 360% since starting business coaching with Clay Clark! We have gone from not showing up in Google search results to coming up first in our city for window cleaning. Before working with Clay Clark we really didn't have a sales system. Having a sales system is helping us to be consistent."

– BRIAN & LINDSAY MUKABI
(Founder of APerfectClean.Net)

"We started business coaching with Clay Clark 120 days ago. From now to then, it is insane. We have increased by 1,000%. We went from 2 calls per week to 20 calls per week."

– JAKE GIBSON
(Founder of RoofAngel.com)

"The Clay Clark business conferences are very filled with knowledge. Clay Clark's business coaching has helped our ministry grow on many social media platforms. The results are real. It has grown our platforms very much."

– AMANDA GRACE
(Founder of www.ArkOfGrace.org)

CHAPTER 03

P

PRIORITY
OPTIMIZING

To be successful in business and life, learning to prioritize the needle-moving activities is crucial. If everything is important, nothing is important. My friend, being present is a present, and you must find some way to be present when it comes to working ON your business and not just working IN your business. In order to thrive financially and to not just survive, you must become a master of time management. Find the time needed to proactively grow your business and to not just reactively deal with the chaos that the life of a business owner will throw at you by default.

NOTABLE QUOTABLE

"Being present is a present and every day is a gift."

- CLAY CLARK

NOTABLE QUOTABLE

"The key is not to prioritize what's on your schedule, but to schedule your priorities."

- STEPHEN COVEY
(An American educator, author, businessman, and keynote speaker. His most popular book was the New York Times best-selling book, The 7 Habits of Highly Effective People.)

You must learn to focus on your business and not just the perpetual "busyness." Just because you got invited to a big event doesn't mean that you have to go. In order to achieve massive success you must become very comfortable with "Saying No to Grow."

NOTABLE QUOTABLE

"There is nothing so useless as doing efficiently
that which should not be done at all."

- PETER DRUCKER

*(The legendary management expert whose 39 books have been
translated into more than thirty-six languages.)*

In order to grow a successful business you must find the time needed to knock out the following action items with excellence:

> Step 1 - Establish Your Revenue Goals

> Step 2 - Determine Your Break-Even Numbers

> Step 3 - Define the Number of Hours Per Week You Are Willing to Work

> Step 4 - Define Your Unique Value Proposition

> Step 5 - Improve Branding

> Step 6 - Create 3-Legged Marketing Stool & a Powerful No-Brainer

> Step 7 - Create a Sales Conversion System

> Step 8 - Determine Sustainable Customer Acquisition Costs

> Step 9 - Create Repeatable Systems, Processes & File Organization

> Step 10 - Create Management Execution Systems

> Step 11 - Create a Sustainable & Repetitive Weekly Schedule

> Step 12 - Create Human Resources & Recruitment Systems

> Step 13 - Create Accounting & Automate Earning Millions

> Step 14 - Determine the Point of Achieving Financial Success

NOTABLE QUOTABLE

"Most people spend more time planning a vacation than they do planning a life."

- CHET HOLMES

(The legendary business consultant and the best-selling author of The Ultimate Sales Machine. Chet Holmes was a business associate of Warren Buffet's business partner, Charlie Munger.)

NOTABLE QUOTABLE

"My reason for teaming up with Clay Clark to write this book is to encourage you if you are simply willing to implement the turn-key and proven plans outlined in this book, you will have massive success. If you will simply invest the time and money needed to find wise counsel, a proven mentor, an accountability partner or program of some kind, you too can have massive success. My speciality is fitness, so that is what I am focused on. But regardless of what area of life you are looking to experience success in, I sincerely believe that you need a mentor for many reasons, but PRIORITY OPTIMIZING is absolutely critical. We are all super busy. We all have just 24 hours in a given day, yet you and I must find a way to focus on PRIORITY OPTIMIZING, you must schedule time to focus on what matters, and to simply not schedule time to do what doesn't matter."

- COLTON CLAUSSEN
(The Founder of www.ClaussenTulsaPersonalTraining.com)

Having worked directly with thousands of entrepreneurs to help them achieve massive success, I have consistently found that by default, most entrepreneurs are engaged in perpetual "busyness" that does not help them to grow their business. As an entrepreneur, you must discover the CORE REPEATABLE ACTIONABLE PROCESSES and the REVENUE PRODUCING ACTIVITIES that will drive you and your company to super success. As an example, when working with Christina Nemes and her company www.CapecodAutobodyAndDetailing.com to help them achieve 170% growth within a very short period of time, we had to teach Christina and her team to master the execution of the following CORE REPEATABLE ACTIONABLE PROCESSES:

1. Gather Real Objective Video Reviews from Real Customers

2. Gather Images of Real Projects That She and Her Team Were Really Working On

3. Writing 500 Words of Original HTML (Hypertext Markup Language) Content Every Day for Her Website

4. Gather Objective Google Reviews from Real Clients

5. Execute the Dream 100 Marketing to Her Ideal & Likely Referral Sources

6. Implement the Group Interview to Find, Hire, Inspire, Train, and Retain Quality Employees

7. Hold Daily Huddles to Start the Day Right and to Hold People Accountable for Delivering the Results Related to Their Jobs

8. Host a Weekly All-Staff Meeting to Share the Vision for the Company, to Celebrate Wins and to Verify That the Company Was Not Drifting

9. Diligently Track Key Performance Indicators to Verify That the Sales, the Profits, and the Core Revenue Producing Activities Were Taking Place

10. Update the Website to Adhere to All of Google's Search Engine Optimization Requirements

11. Role Play and Train On Call Scripting So That Inbound Leads Turn Into Happy Paying Customers

12. Simplify the operations and workflow on a weekly basis.

13. Analyze the metrics that impacted her business to prevent drifting and to increase productivity and profitability.

NOTABLE QUOTABLE

"Implementation, not ideas, is the key to real success."

- CHET HOLMES

(The legendary business consultant and the best-selling author of The Ultimate Sales Machine.)

Implementing the action items above repeatedly with diligence and mastery is what grew Christina's business. Action that generates traction is what grew the business 170% within just eighteen months. However, in order to find the time to get the action items listed above completed every week, Christina and every other successful entrepreneur that I have ever had to work with had to stop doing action items that were not related to the Core Revenue Producing Activities.

NOTABLE QUOTABLE

"Action is the real measure of intelligence."

- NAPOLEON HILL
(The legendary best-selling author of the number one most read self-help book of all-time, Think and Grow Rich.)

In order to get unstuck and take your business and your life to the next level, YOU MUST BLOCK OUT TIME EVERY DAY to plan your day. As you plan your day, ask yourself what action steps you need to take in order to move closer to the achievement of your goals in the following areas:

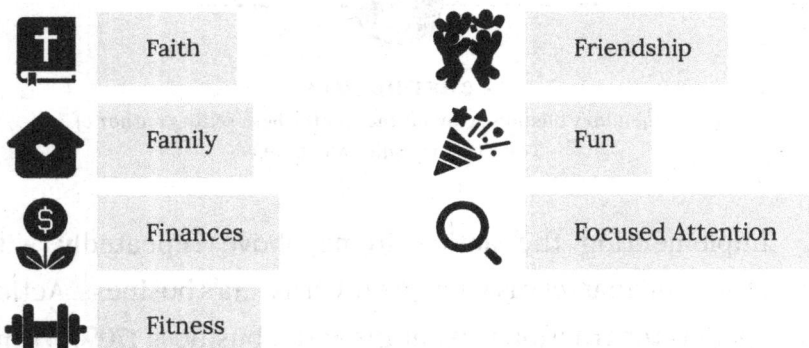

Faith

Friendship

Family

Fun

Finances

Focused Attention

Fitness

NOTABLE QUOTABLE

"Either you run the day or the day runs you."

- JIM ROHN

(The legendary self-help guru, best-selling author and sales trainer who taught millions of people how to become more productive and successful in their lives. Jim Rohn's writing and speaking influenced an entire generation of self-help authors and speakers.)

When you begin to intentionally design your day rather than just reacting to the world around you, you will begin to develop traction. When you find a proven mentor or coaching program, they will help you to identify your REVENUE PRODUCING ACTIVITIES and the CORE REPEATABLE ACTIONABLE PROCESSES that will help you move closer to the achievement of your goals on a daily basis. If you have any ambition at all, you are probably already experiencing "busyness," but you need you to block out time to work on your life instead of just cluttering your day with busyness.

NOTABLE QUOTABLE

"Concentrate all your thoughts upon the work in hand. The sun's rays do not burn until brought to a focus."

- ALEXANDER GRAHAM BELL
(The inventor of the first practical telephone and the co-founder of AT&T, American Telephone and Telegraph Company.)

NOTABLE QUOTABLE

"You must take personal responsibility. You cannot change the circumstances, the seasons, or the wind, but you can change yourself. That is something you are in charge of."

- JIM ROHN
(The legendary self-help guru, best-selling author and sales trainer who taught millions of people how to become more productive and successful in their lives.)

What is "busyness"? Busyness means you are perpetually busy but you won't know "Y."

What is business? Business means that you are working diligently on the CORE REPEATABLE ACTIONABLE PROCESSES that will help you ("I") become successful.

Over the years, having hired some of the best consultants on the planet, I can tell you that learning the right things to do can be frustrating when you have been investing copious amounts of time doing the wrong things. I remember when I hired Bruce Clay of www.BruceClay.com to teach me search engine optimization and I remember paying $8,000 per month. As I look back at this time in my life objectively, I realize that I was paying one of the world's most respected search engine optimization experts to teach me how to optimize the websites for our businesses, and yet I didn't want to hear what he was teaching.

I was paying Bruce over $8,000 per month to teach me search engine optimization, and I didn't want to hear that I needed to write 1,000 words of original content per page of my website while weaving in the keyword that I was trying to optimize for six times per 1,000 words. I didn't want to hear that the websites we had built didn't have the correct XML sitemap and HTML sitemap. I wanted Bruce Clay to tell me that we were doing everything correctly and that we were on the right path, but in fact we were 100% on the wrong path and we needed to dramatically change the daily CORE REPEATABLE ACTIONABLE PROCESSES that we were implementing if we ever wanted to achieve traction and massive success. Bruce, thank you for teaching us the right way to optimize websites.

NOTABLE QUOTABLE

"Lazy hands make for poverty, but diligent hands bring wealth."

PROVERBS 10:4
(From the controversial book known as The Bible)

I am asking you right now. Are you going in the right direction with your life? Are you getting closer to the achievement of your goals or are you drifting around going the wrong direction or even diligently and aggressively going the wrong direction? Are you producing traction from the action that you are taking or are you just filling your calendar with perpetual "busyness"? If you believe that you are going 90 miles per hour in the wrong direction, you are probably in need of an inspection of your daily calendar, your daily action steps, and a serious course correction. That is what a proven mentor and coaching program will do for you.

NOTABLE QUOTABLE

"If you don't design your own life plan, chances are you'll fall into someone else's plan. And guess what they have planned for you? Not much."

- JIM ROHN
(The legendary self-help guru, best-selling author and sales trainer who taught millions of people how to become more productive and successful in their lives.)

When I work with clients to help them achieve real success, I have found that successful entrepreneurs need to know what to do, how to do it, and they need someone to hold them accountable to actually turning their "To-Do List" into a "Done List." Once you have identified the CORE REPEATABLE ACTIONABLE PROCESSES that you and your business need to implement on a daily basis, you must work with a sense of urgency, because life is not a dress rehearsal.

NOTABLE QUOTABLE

"Without a sense of urgency, desire
loses its value."

- JIM ROHN

*(The legendary self-help guru, best-selling author and sales
trainer who taught millions of people how to become more
productive and successful in their lives.)*

Something powerful happens when you know what to do and you are held accountable to actually doing it. Life-changing momentum begins to occur once you have a proven mentor or coaching program in your life. Being coached aggressively helps you identify what is not working so that you can stop wasting your time on what cannot and will not ever produce positive traction or gain results in your life. My friend, this is the year to stop doing what doesn't work and to start doing what does work.

CELEBRATING THE 800% GROWTH OF REAL CLAY CLARK BUSINESS COACHING CLIENT SUCCESS STORY - WWW.NEWCONCEPT.HEALTHCARE

"I was listening to different podcasts about business. We were looking to start our business and I started listening to you. I got on your website and I was just a little girl starting a business and I thought I'm going to ask this guy to be my coach. Our website is www.NewConcept. Healcare. We are functional medicine. It was pretty overwhelming and we were starting this business with absolutely nothing. You guys have helped us through the growing pains. The website is great. We would have never been able to do that by ourselves. Your marketing gets people into our practice!"

- GINNY & MIKE MINGIONI, THE CO-FOUNDERS OF NEWCONCEPT.HEALTHCARE

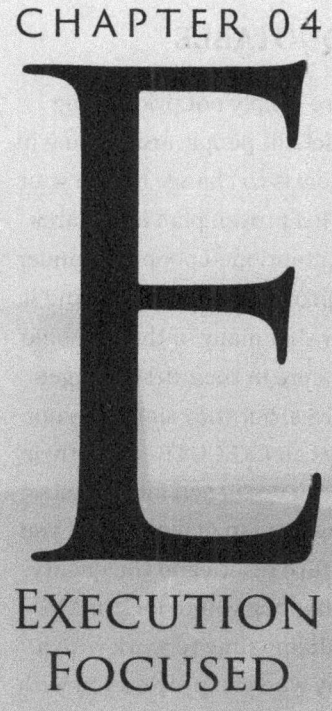

CHAPTER 04

E

EXECUTION
FOCUSED

Oftentimes I find that well-intentioned people who choose to become entrepreneurs like talking, chit-chatting, light-hearted banter, BS-ing, having a good time, and engaging in unproductive, yet fun conversation. However, if we keep this up, it will lead to poverty.

NOTABLE QUOTABLE

"Ideas are easy. Implementation is hard."

- GUY KAWASAKI

(Multiple-time www.ThrivetimeShow.com podcast guest, and best-selling author, speaker, entrepreneur and evangelist. He is the chief evangelist of Canva, an online graphic design tool, a brand ambassador for Mercedes-Benz and an executive fellow of the Haas School of Business (UC Berkeley).)

NOTABLE QUOTABLE

"By default, most people are simply not prioritizing fitness in their lives, thus by default people are drifting in the area of their fitness. My goal is to change that in your life and to help you EXECUTE a proven plan in the area of fitness. I see so many well intentioned people meander into a gym without having a proven plan to follow, and it frustrates me because I know that many of these people are well intentioned and sincere in their desire to get into the best shape of their lives, but they simply do not know a proven plan that they can EXECUTE. Thus, their intentions often are not able to be turned into results. To motivate you and encourage you to make the BIG and RIGHT decisions for your future health and the quality of your life, I have done all but beg you to lock in and completely commit to scheduling time to work with a trainer, a mentor or somebody who can provide you with wise counsel, accountability and motivation in the area of fitness over the next 45 days! Will you do it? I know that you can. I believe in you, but the choice is yours."

- COLTON CLAUSSEN
(The Founder of www.ClaussenTulsaPersonalTraining.com)

NOTABLE QUOTABLE

"In all labor there is profit, But idle chatter leads only to poverty."

PROVERBS 14:23

This chapter might not be the most fun chapter that the world has ever produced, but it is true. A proven mentor or coaching program will make sure that you are getting things done and not just talking about getting things done. Many years ago, I met a man by the name of Aaron Antis. At the time, Aaron was the marketing director for www.ShawHomes.com and had already achieved big-time success before he hired me to grow www.ShawHomes.com. However, in order for him and I to grow www.ShawHomes.com from $14 million per year in annual sales to $140 million per year in annual sales, we had to diligently implement the REVENUE PRODUCING CORE REPEATABLE ACTIONABLE PROCESSES that I knew would produce massive success. Thus, Aaron and I spent 90% of our meetings focused on identifying things that needed to be done, implementing the best-practice systems, and solving any problems that were preventing us from achieving the business growth we were focused on.

"I'M A GREAT BELIEVER IN LUCK, AND I FIND THE HARDER I WORK, THE MORE I HAVE OF IT."
– THOMAS JEFFERSON

NOTABLE QUOTABLE

"It's a no-brainer. We get more leads than we can handle. We've got different problems now. There are franchises in town and they have marketing budgets and we are now able to do better than they are. What you are doing with the marketing is outdoing what they are doing. You have taught us that you will slack where you don't track. The business coaching keeps me from procrastinating. They keep me on schedule and accountable. It's very much worth what I pay. You've got it all broken up into different categories...you've got the marketing, the sales, the management and your 14 steps that we are going through. You've created a template and someone holding you accountable for those things. It makes it a lot easier. I graduated from college, it's not like I don't know how to read. You've already got the system developed, it's just easier. It's an absolute no-brainer. You have quality coaches. We worked 10 years in a different franchise and their system sucked compared to what Clay Clark is coaching me. We went on a cruise for the first time since our honeymoon and that was fun! We are stepping into this thing where we are now actually enjoying a vacation here or there."

- JEAN HENDRYX
(Founder of SafeTransportMoving.com)

Although the meetings were friendly and Aaron and I had become good friends, we didn't spend our meetings talking in circles about feelings, current events, and random things that made us both laugh. Aaron diligently implemented what I taught him, and I diligently focused the weekly meeting times on identifying what needed to be done, discussing how to implement what needed to be done, and to solving the problems that were keeping the company from growing faster.

NOTABLE QUOTABLE

"ACTA NON VERBA is the motto of the U.S. Merchant Marine Academy. Don't listen to what a person says, watch what they do."

- ROBERT KIYOSAKI

(Robert Kiyosaki is an international best-selling author of the Rich Dad Poor Dad book series, a legendary real estate investor, multiple-time ThrivetimeShow.com podcast guest, and entrepreneur. Kiyosaki is the author of more than 26 books, including the international self-published personal finance Rich Dad Poor Dad series of books which has been translated into 51 languages and sold over 41 million copies worldwide.)

NOTABLE QUOTABLE

"That's been one of my mantras – focus and simplicity. Simple can be harder than complex: You have to work hard to get your thinking clean to make it simple. But it's worth it in the end because once you get there, you can move mountains."

- STEVE JOBS

(The man who personally led the charge to make personal computers that non-nerds could use, the man who co-founded Apple, the man who introduced the first 100% digitally animated box office success story (Toy Story) when he was the CEO of the company. The man who revolutionized the music industry with the iPod and iTunes. The man who introduced the iPad tablet technology to the planet and the man who introduced the game-changing phone, the iPhone, to the planet. He was a dude who got things done.)

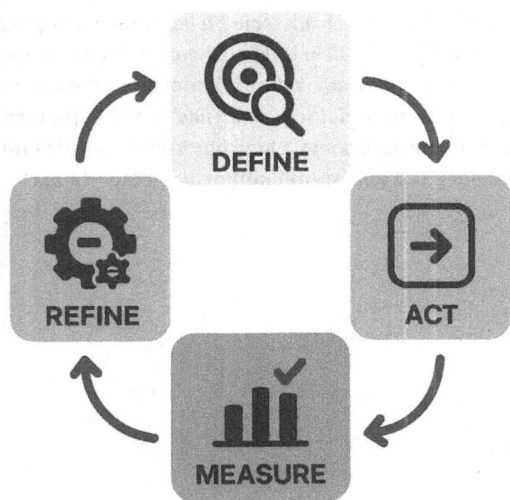

In order to succeed as an entrepreneur, you and I must embrace the rhythm and cadence of entrepreneurship. What is this cadence? This cadence consists of:

 Define - You must define what you believe or know is going to work.

 Act - You must hold yourself and your team accountable for actually implementing and taking the action steps needed to implement your plan.

 Measure - You must fastidiously and diligently track your results. You must measure what you treasure, because by default, you will slack where you do not track.

 Refine - You must refine and iterate each and every week based upon tracking your KEY PERFORMANCE INDICATORS if you want to generate momentum and success as an entrepreneur.

NOTABLE QUOTABLE

"The difference between great people and everyone else is that great people create their lives actively, while everyone else is created by their lives, passively waiting to see where life takes them next. The difference between the two is living fully and just existing."

- MICHAEL GERBER
(The best-selling author of The E-Myth book series, the legendary entrepreneur and multiple-time www.ThrivetimeShow.com podcast guest.)

What? Yes! You must master the rhythm of entrepreneurship and the cadence of SUPER SUCCESS if you want to become a successful entrepreneur and grow a successful and scalable business model.

NOTABLE QUOTABLE

"Most entrepreneurs are merely technicians with an entrepreneurial seizure. Most entrepreneurs fail because you are working IN your business rather than ON your business."

- MICHAEL GERBER
(The best-selling author of The E-Myth book series, the legendary entrepreneur and multiple-time www.ThrivetimeShow.com podcast guest.)

As an example, for many years, I have had the pleasure to work with a brand called www.OXIFresh.com based in Denver, Colorado. The founder of the company, Jonathan Barnett has been a long-time friend of mine, and over the years, the brand has now opened over 500 locations! How?

In the world of franchising, the vast majority of franchises are sold through a network of franchise coaches (who are similar to brokers in the world of real estate). Because of how they market to potential franchisees (whom they call "Seekers"), these franchise coaches talk to many people who simply want to find and buy the best franchise (Thus, if you want to sell franchises, it is a good idea for you to become friends with the franchise coach community).

NOTABLE QUOTABLE

"Most people are sitting on their own diamond mines. The surest ways to lose your diamond mine is to get bored, become overambitious, or start thinking that the grass is greener on the other side. Find your core focus, stick to it, and devote your time and resources to excelling at it."

- GINO WICKMAN
(The legendary business growth consultant, best-selling author and multiple time www.ThrivetimeShow.com Podcast guest.)

One of the most well known and successful franchise coaches in the history of franchising is a man by the name of Terry Powell. Thus, I doggedly pursued Terry Powell and introduced him to the Oxi Fresh franchising team. It took a long time to get in contact with Terry Powell, to interview him multiple times on the www.ThrivetimeShow.com podcast, and to ultimately introduce him to the www.OXIFresh.com team, but that is exactly what I did.

That one move, that one connection, and that one implemented action step forever changed the game for www.OXIFresh.com franchising. And although I loved working with the wonderful www.OXIFresh.com team over the years, it was that connection to Terry Powell and his fabulous team of franchise coaches that moved the needle when it came to generating franchising leads and potential buyers of the www.OXIFresh.com franchise. What am I saying? I am saying that EXECUTING ON THE PROVEN PLAN IS ULTIMATELY WHAT IS MOST IMPORTANT.

NOTABLE QUOTABLE

"You either pay now or pay later with just about every decision you make about where and how you spend your time."

- LEE COCKERELL

(A multiple-time www.ThrivetimeShow.com Podcast guest, the former Executive Vice President of Walt Disney World Resorts who once managed 40,000 employees and over 1 million customers (guests) per week. Clay Clark assisted Lee Cockerell in writing the best-selling book, Time Management Magic.)

As another example, I have had the opportunity and pleasure of working with Dave & Tricia Rich with www. Pappagallos.com, www.MorningGloryEatery.com and www. BeachesAndCreamSB.com for nearly 8 years. During those incredible years working together, we have nearly grown their gross revenue by 8 times. How? As their coach, I focused on the EXECUTION and diligently executing the proven plan and success strategies that I know will work when it comes to growing, expanding, and scaling restaurants. Dave and Tricia were diligent doers, and they were willing to put in the work, but they needed to be shown the proven plan and how to implement it.

In order to grow a successful business, I knew Tricia and Dave had to make the time needed to knock out the following action items with excellence:

> **Step 1** - Establish Your Revenue Goals

> **Step 2** - Determine Your Break-Even Numbers

> **Step 3** - Define the Number of Hours Per Week You Are Willing to Work

> **Step 4** - Define Your Unique Value Proposition

> **Step 5** - Improve Branding

> **Step 6** - Create 3-Legged Marketing Stool & a Powerful No-Brainer

> **Step 7** - Create a Sales Conversion System

> **Step 8** - Determine Sustainable Customer Acquisition Costs

> **Step 9** - Create Repeatable Systems, Processes & File Organization

> **Step 10** - Create Management Execution Systems

> **Step 11** - Create a Sustainable & Repetitive Weekly Schedule

> **Step 12** - Create Human Resources & Recruitment Systems

> **Step 13** - Create Accounting & Automate Earning Millions

> **Step 14** - Determine the Point of Achieving Financial Success

I knew that Dave and Tricia needed to introduce a compelling customer experience that involved optimizing the sights, the sounds, the smells, the atmosphere, and the overall experience of their incredible Satellite Beach, Florida restaurant. To their credit, Dave and Tricia Rich were willing to put in the work needed to wow their customers day after day with a spirit of excellence. Although we have had fun together growing their businesses over the years, our entire focus during each meeting was to diligently execute the proven plan because people pay us to help them grow their business not to simply pontificate about business theories and concepts that could work.

NOTABLE QUOTABLE

"Simple can be harder than complex: You have to work hard to get your thinking clean to make it simple. But it's worth it in the end because once you get there, you can move mountains."

- STEVE JOBS

(The man who revolutionized the personal computer, recorded audio, telecommunications and animated movie industries. Steve Jobs co-founded Apple, turned around PIXAR while serving as their CEO and founded a company called NeXT which created an operating system that was later acquired by Apple).

My entire focus as a business coach is making sure that my clients generate more revenue than they are paying me as quickly as possible by diligently implementing proven processes and success systems that have been proven to work. However, if a system or a business growth strategy is too complex, it will simply not work because it cannot be implemented. As you grow your business, you must keep in mind that simplicity scales and complexity fails.

My friend, the reality is that many of the most well-intentioned people around us will unintentionally keep us poor by validating our ideas that will not work, encouraging us to do things that don't make sense, and filling our minds and our days with idle conversation that will lead to poverty. In order to achieve massive success you need to find a proven mentor or coaching program that puts focus on being EXECUTION FOCUSED and on achieving the goals you have for your life.

"Worry, Lack of Confidence, Bashfulness, Irresolution, Timidity, Depression, and all the rest of the negative family of feelings and emotions are the progeny of Fear. Without Fear none of these minor emotions or feelings would exist. By killing off the parent of this brood of mental vampires, you escape the coming generations of negative thoughts, and thus keep your Mental Attitude gardens free from these pests and nuisances."

- NAPOLEON HILL
(The life-changing and best-selling author of Think & Grow Rich. Clay Clark named his son Aubrey Napoleon-Hill Clark after Napoleon Hill.)

THE WEATHER CHANNEL UNPLUGGED:
LET GO OF WHAT YOU CAN'T CONTROL

"GREAT SPIRITS HAVE ALWAYS ENCOUNTERED VIOLENT OPPOSITION FROM MEDIOCRE MINDS."
- ALBERT EINSTEIN

CELEBRATING THE 11X GROWTH OF REAL CLAY CLARK BUSINESS COACHING CLIENT SUCCESS STORY, AARON ANTIS OF SHAWHOMES.COM

"The interesting thing is our internet leads from our website in four month period of time has gone from 10-15 leads in a month to 180 internet leads in a month just from the few things that he showed us how to implement that I would have never come up with on my own so I have alot of good things to say about the system that Clay Clark (created) and put in place with us and it has just been an incredible experience. I think in the 35-year history of ShawHomes.com, Clay Clark is probably the best thing that has happened to us and I know that if you give him a shot I think you'll feel the same way. I know for me the thing that I would have missed out on if I didn't work with Clay Clark is I would have missed out on literally an 1,800% increase in our internet leads...from 10 leads per month to 180 leads per month.

Honestly, I kind of thought that I knew everything about marketing and homes and then I met Clay Clark, and my perception of what I knew and what I could do definitely changed. After doing $800 million in sales over a 15-year career, I really thought I knew what I was doing. I've been managing a large team of sales people over the last 10 years with ShawHomes.com and we have been a company that has been in business for 35 years.

We've become one of the largest builders in the area. I'm very glad that we met and had the opportunity to work with Clay Clark. So the interaction with Clay Clark on a weekly basis is honestly very enlightening. One of the things that I love about Clay Clark's perspective is that he doesn't come from my industry. I've listened to all the experts in our field, our company has paid for me to go to seminars, international builder shows and all sorts of experts in our industry, but the thing that I've found working with Clay Clark is that he has a perspective that is very valuable time every week when I get that hour with him. The results that we've gotten in a very short period of time are honestly MONUMENTAL and Clay Clark has exceeded my wildest expectation of what he might be able to do. I came in skeptical because I am very pragmatic and as I've gone through the process over just a few months I've realized it's probably one of the best moves we've ever made. I think alot of people think they don't need a business coach because they like to think they know everything. I know that is the way I felt coming in. We are a big company that is definitely one of the largest in town. I think alot of people let their ego get in the way of listening to somebody that may have a better perspective than theirs. I would absolutely recommend Clay Clark. I guarantee you are not going to regret it because we sure haven't."

- AARON ANTIS
(Marketing Director of ShawHomes.com and Co-Founder of KingdomBCG.com)

"When the light pours in, the darkness disappears. So it is with the darkness of Fear -- throw open the windows, and "let a little sunshine in." Let the thoughts, feelings, and ideals of Courage, Confidence, and Fearlessness pour into your mind, and Fear will vanish. Whenever Fear shows itself in your mind, administer the antidote of Fearlessness immediately. Say to yourself: 'I am Fearless; I Fear Nothing; I am Courageous.' Let the sunshine pour in."

- NAPOLEON HILL
(The life-changing and best-selling author of Think & Grow Rich. Clay Clark named his son Aubrey Napoleon-Hill Clark after Napoleon Hill.)

CHAPTER 05

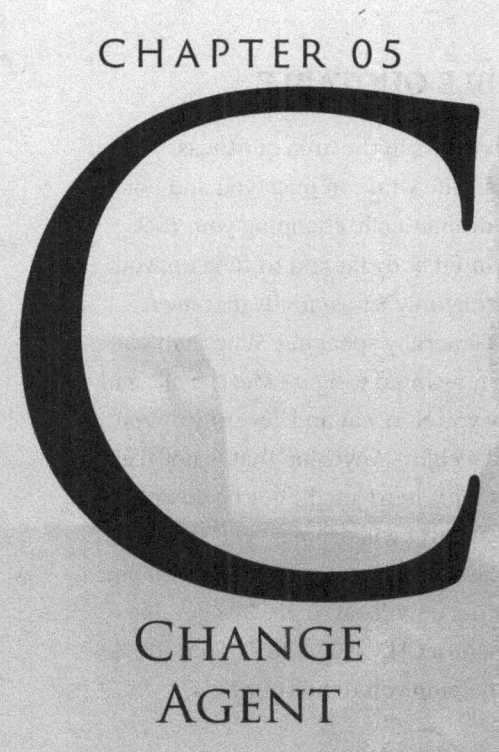

CHANGE AGENT

In route to helping thousands of entrepreneurs to build successful companies, I have found that most people need an outside catalyst, a sparkplug, motivator, activator, implementor, or CHANGE AGENT, because most people are not looking for a breakthrough until they are on the verge of a breakdown. Why? I don't know.

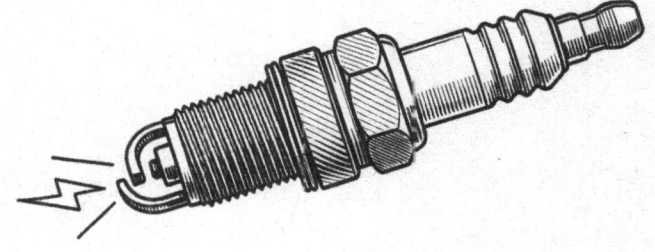

NOTABLE QUOTABLE

"In order to achieve results in the area of fitness, you need somebody in your life who can push you and hold you accountable to dramatically changing your diet. In order to lose unwanted body fat and to tone up, you must commit to eating only whole foods diet meat, vegetables and fruit. Generally speaking. What can you eat if you want to lose unwanted weight? Meat, fruit, and vegetables. What can you NOT eat and consume if you want to lose unwanted weight? Anything that is not fruit, vegetables, and meat. This news might not be complex or highly-motivational, but I will promise you that you will lose massive amounts of weight and feel better if you simply commit to eating only meat, fruit, & vegetables over the next 45 days. As a CHANGE AGENT I am 100% obsessed with helping you to be your best."

- COLTON CLAUSSEN
(The Founder of www.ClaussenTulsaPersonalTraining.com)

NOTABLE QUOTABLE

"Knowledge is the key that unlocks all the doors. You can be green-skinned with yellow polka dots and come from Mars, but if you have knowledge that people need, instead of beating you, they'll beat a path to your door."

- BEN CARSON

(A ThrivetimeShow.com Podcast guest, an American retired neurosurgeon, academic, author, and government official who served as the 17th United States secretary of housing and urban development from 2017 to 2021. A pioneer in the field of neurosurgery, he was a candidate for President of the United States in the 2016 Republican primaries. Carson is one of the most prominent black conservatives in the United States.)

I've found that many business owners by default will simply not hold their team accountable to implementing best-practice strategies, tracking numbers, completing jobs on time, sticking within a budget, following sales scripts, wowing customers, or following proven systems. They would rather be liked by poor performing teammates than become successful. You and I need someone in our life that will serve as that CHANGE AGENT and the catalyst to push us out of our comfort zone and into the high profitability zone.

I find that even when most entrepreneurs learn specifically what they need to do to start and grow a successful business, they often struggle to implement what they know they should be doing within their business. This could be because they don't want to offend their employees, upset their teammates, hold their team accountable, or cause any kind of disagreement or conflict. This is why you need a CHANGE AGENT in your life. When you replace systems that DON'T work with systems that DO work, you need an implementer and a change agent to help you successfully implement the proven systems.

My friend, no one drifts to success. You need a CHANGE AGENT in your life who will motivate, support, and guide you during the time of transition from dysfunction into function. You and I need someone in our life that will serve as that CHANGE AGENT and the catalyst to push us out of our comfort zone and into the high profitability zone.

NOTABLE QUOTABLE

"When you want to succeed as bad as you want to breathe, then you'll be successful."

- ERIC THOMAS
(A *www.ThrivetimeShow.com* Podcast guest, *motivational speaker, author, and consultant.*)

NOTABLE QUOTABLE

"A person's success in life can usually be measured by the number of uncomfortable conversations he or she is willing to have."

- TIM FERRISS
(Best-selling author, investor, podcaster, and entrepreneur.)

NOTABLE QUOTABLE

"The last three or four reps is what makes the muscle grow. This area of pain divides the champion from someone else who is not a champion. That's what most people lack, having the guts to go on and just say they'll go through the pain no matter what happens."

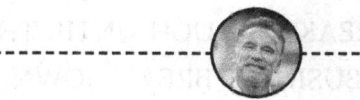

- ARNOLD SCHWARZENEGGER
(The 38th Governor for the state of California who won the Mr. Universe title at the age of 20 and who went on to win the Mr. Olympia contest seven times. Arnold also has achieved success as an actor, a businessman, and politician.)

"FACE REALITY AS IT IS, NOT AS IT WAS OR AS YOU WISH IT TO BE."
– JACK WELCH

The pattern and reality that I have witnessed time and time again is that most business owners and people are not looking for a BIG BUSINESS BREAKTHROUGH UNTIL THEY ARE ON THE VERGE OF A BIG BUSINESS BREAK DOWN. This is why I firmly believe that you and I need a proactive and persistent change agent in our lives and in our businesses to push our companies and ourselves to make the changes we need to make before we have to.

NOTABLE QUOTABLE

"Mentors, by far, are the most important aspects of businesses."

- DAYMOND JOHN

(A www.ThrivetimeShow.com Podcast guest, the founder of FUBU. Daymond John is an investor on the ABC reality television series Shark Tank. He is the founder, president, and chief executive officer of FUBU, and is the founder of The Shark Group. To make ends meet, John held a full-time job at Red Lobster, working on the FUBU business in between shifts.)

We live in the information age, thus we all get great ideas from YouTube, podcasts, business books, business gurus, conferences, seminars, workshops, and occasionally from formal education. However, I have found consistently that IMPLEMENTATION is the missing factor for most people and businesses. In order to implement and apply the proven processes, best-practice business building strategies, and success systems, you need to learn how to be persistent and to follow up with your team until the job gets done. You need to follow up until the action item gets completed and until the proven processes and success systems that you are learning are being implemented with excellence. Learning the best-practice success systems and proven processes is important, but it's all about implementation—which is why I find that everyone needs a CHANGE AGENT.

Why do ordinary men and women get into great physical shape when they join the military and survive basic training and bootcamp? It's accountability, it's coaching, and it's having a CHANGE AGENT in their life that will push them to be their best.

I have found that the vast majority of business people on the planet Earth (perhaps this is different on other planets) struggle to make a decision on which strategies are the PROVEN systems that they should implement. At the same time, many business owners who know what strategies to implement STILL struggle to implement the proven systems in their businesses. Growing a business is NOT about consistently chasing new ideas all the time, it's about implementation.

NOTABLE QUOTABLE

"Most people want to avoid pain, and discipline is usually painful."

- JOHN MAXWELL

(A multiple-time www.ThrivetimeShow.com Podcast guest, best-selling author, speaker, and pastor who has written many books, primarily focusing on leadership. John Maxwell is best known for his best-selling books which include The 21 Irrefutable Laws of Leadership and The 21 Indispensable Qualities of a Leader. Many of John Maxwell's books have been on the New York Times Best Seller list.)

You and I need a CHANGE AGENT in our life that will act like the pressure that turns carbon into a diamond. Diamonds are only made up of one element, and that is carbon. When carbon dioxide is buried approximately 100 miles under the Earth's surface, heated to a temperature of 2,200 degrees Fahrenheit, and then squeezed to a pressure of 725,000 lb per square inch, a diamond is formed.

NOTABLE QUOTABLE

"Confidence comes from discipline and training."

- ROBERT KIYOSAKI

(The legendary author of The Rich Dad Poor Dad book series, the successful investor, iconic podcaster, prolific educator and multiple time www.ThrivetimeShow.com Podcast guest.)

You and I need a CHANGE AGENT in our life that will act as the perpetual and repetitive heating source that turns water into boiling water. Water boils at 212° Fahrenheit. If the water is 100°, it is hot. If the water is 200°, it is very hot. However, water will not boil until it reaches 212°. Most people need someone that pushes them over and over until they reach that boiling point where figuratively speaking they change dramatically from one state to another. Boiling water kills or inactivates viruses, bacteria, protozoa, and other pathogens by using heat to damage structural components and disrupt essential life processes (e.g. denature proteins), however hot water cannot do this.

Perhaps these analogies are not impacting you in a positive way, and that is fine. The point is, YOU NEED SOMEONE THAT WILL PUSH YOU TO IMPLEMENT PROVEN SYSTEMS AND TO SERVE AS YOUR CHANGE AGENT, OR YOU WILL STAY STUCK.

NOTABLE QUOTABLE

"Persistence trumps talent. What's the most powerful force in the universe? Compound interest. It builds on itself. Over time, a small amount of money becomes a large amount of money. Persistence is similar. A little bit improves performance, which encourages greater persistence, which improves persistence even more. And on and on it goes. Lack of persistence works the same way -- only in the opposite direction."

- DANIEL PINK

(A *www.ThrivetimeShow.com Podcast guest, a seven times New York Times bestseller, and the host and a co-executive producer of the National Geographic Channel social science TV series Crowd Control.*)

As humans, we will not ever become great at implementing a given task or system without persistent repetition. As an example, as I am writing this portion of the book, I am sitting in a chair overlooking people playing golf at the incredible Turnberry Golf Course in Scotland. Yesterday, we ran into a golfer that is one of the best golfers in the history of the Turnberry golf course.

He was obsessively working to improve his golf game, even though he was already a professional. Did this man become great at golfing simply by reading books about becoming a skilled golfer? No. Did this man become great at golfing simply by learning new ideas about how to improve

Pictured above is Trump Hotel & Resort located at Maidens Rd, Turnberry, Maidens, Girvan KA26 9LT. United Kingdom.

his golf swing? No. Did this man become a world-class golf-ball wacker guy by simply listening to podcasts about hitting a golf-ball or by attending conferences focused on how to hit the golf ball accurately from point A to point B? No. This man became one of the best golfers at Scotland's Trump Turnberry golf course by practicing hitting the golf ball day after day whether it was cold, rainy, foggy or pleasant outside. This man demonstrated massive levels of persistence and commitment in order to become a great golfer. Learning how to become a professional golfer, or even just a good golfer, requires tremendous discipline, focus and commitment.

Growing a business requires tremendous discipline, focus and commitment. Thus, having a proven mentor or business coaching program is important to push you and your business to become the best that you can be.

Whether it is becoming great at golf or great at business, it often requires repeating the same proven systems and moves over and over and over until you almost begin to hate the repetition and the focus required to become great at something. You must learn how to bore down when the rest of the world struggles with boredom.

NOTABLE QUOTABLE

To quote myself, as an entrepreneur you must remember: "Inspiration is the reward. Inaction is the giant. Action is the sword."

- CLAY CLARK
(America's most pale male and the co-founder of five human kids and the loyal husband to one incredible wife.)

If you want to become successful in golf or in business you must learn to repeat the proven systems and moves over and over and over and over. Most self-proclaimed business building gurus will preach, "Insanity is doing the same thing over and over and expecting a different result."

I have found that insanity is: "Endlessly trying new ideas, new investments, new strategies, new girlfriends, new wives, new cars, new business ideas, and new business models with the hope that you will eventually find something that isn't 'boring.' To become successful, you must bore down and repeatedly do what needs to be done to produce success, regardless of whether you find the work to be boring, repetitive or tedious."

My friend, once you and your team learn to master the implementation of needle-moving growth strategies and success systems, life will become exciting because your business will be booming and thriving. You MUST learn how to find the pig-headed discipline needed to get the work done.

NOTABLE QUOTABLE

"No one gets good at anything without repetition. Karate requires tremendous discipline. You're just repeating moves over and over. This is true of tennis, golf, or any other sport. Practice, practice, practice, and then, when you've begun to master your moves so that you know what to do automatically, it gets exciting. But pigheaded discipline comes first."

- CHET HOLMES

(The legendary business growth consultant and best-selling author that successfully helped to grow thousands of companies before his early death. Chet Holmes wrote the life-changing book The Ultimate Sales Machine, which every entrepreneur should read.)

As yet another example of a business owner who is now booming as a result of having a CHANGE AGENT in his life, I want to tell you the story about Kevin Thomas. Who is Kevin Thomas? He is the founder of www.MultiCleanOK.com, and we have helped Kevin to grow his business from being stuck at 50 employees to now BOOMING with 350+ employees! How did we help Kevin to grow his business by 7 times? Kevin needed a

CHANGE AGENT in his life to diligently implement the proven plan listed below. Kevin didn't want to move via guesswork, and he wasn't interested in trying strategies that might work. Kevin wanted to implement a plan that WOULD WORK if he was willing to do THE WORK.

> Step 1 - Establish Your Revenue Goals

> Step 2 - Determine Your Break-Even Numbers

> Step 3 - Define the Number of Hours Per Week You Are Willing to Work

> Step 4 - Define Your Unique Value Proposition

> Step 5 - Improve Branding

> Step 6 - Create 3-Legged Marketing Stool & a Powerful No-Brainer

> Step 7 - Create a Sales Conversion System

> Step 8 - Determine Sustainable Customer Acquisition Costs

> Step 9 - Create Repeatable Systems, Processes & File Organization

> Step 10 - Create Management Execution Systems

> Step 11 - Create a Sustainable & Repetitive Weekly Schedule

> Step 12 - Create Human Resources & Recruitment Systems

> Step 13 - Create Accounting & Automate Earning Millions

> Step 14 - Determine the Point of Achieving Financial Success

Week after week, year after year, Kevin had been willing to diligently implement the proven systems and success strategies that we taught him. However, he needed a CHANGE AGENT in the form of a proven mentor and coaching program to help him implement the proven branding, marketing, sales, hiring, management, and accounting systems that have been shown time and time again to produce fruit in the lives of people.

NOTABLE QUOTABLE

"We must all suffer one of two things: the pain of discipline or the pain of regret or disappointment."

- JIM ROHN

(Jim Rohn mentored Mark R. Hughes (the founder of Herbalife International) and the legendary life strategists and self-help guru, Tony Robbins in the late 1970s. Others who credit Rohn for influencing their careers include authors/lecturers Mark Victor Hansen and Jack Canfield (Chicken Soup book series), Everton Edwards (Hallmark Innovators Conglomerate), Brian Tracy, Darren Hardy, Todd Smith, Kevin Garver, T. Harv Eker. Rohn coauthored the novel Twelve Pillars with Chris Widener.)

Why Did Kevin Need A Coach?

Like most people, Kevin needed a coach to push him to the next level just like most people in the military need a drill sergeant to push them to become the elite physical specimens we often find working at the most distinguished levels of the military. Kevin needed a CHANGE AGENT who was willing to have the uncomfortable, and often repetitive, conversations with him on a weekly basis to make sure that he was turning his TO-DO LIST into a TO-DONE LIST. Kevin needed a team to push him to implement the repetitive and tedious search engine strategy to generate more leads. Kevin needed a team to push him to implement the boring, tedious, and mind-numbing online reputation management strategy in order to increase the effectiveness of his DREAM 100 business-to-business marketing strategy to business owners. Kevin needed someone to push him to implement the proven GROUP INTERVIEW employee hiring and recruitment strategy. KEVIN needed someone to followup and harass him about diligently implementing the proven TRACKING SHEET SYSTEM. Kevin needed someone to hound him and follow up about implementing the proven SALE SCRIPTING.

What was the search engine optimization strategy? What is a DREAM 100 business to business marketing strategy? What was the GROUP INTERVIEW hiring strategy? These are all proven systems that we teach at our in-person www.ThrivetimeShow.com business growth conferences, on our www.ThrivetimeShow.com business podcasts and directly to our 160 one-on-one business coaching clients.

It is all about IMPLEMENTATION and not just CONVERSATION.

It is all about IMPLEMENTATION and not just the MENTAL constipation caused by the endless EDUCATION related to our OCCUPATION. My friend, success is all about IMPLEMENTATION, and unless you are one of the most unique humans to have ever lived on the planet Earth, you are going to need a CHANGE AGENT and a catalyst in your life to help you turn your dreams into reality.

REVENUE GROWTH AFTER WORKING WITH CLAY CLARK

- 2018 — $1,503,388.89
- 2019 — $1,705,831.29
- 2020 — $1,795,257.36
- 2021 — $2,331,378.37

"DILIGENCE, COACHABILITY, AND ATTENTION TO DETAIL ARE THE DIFFERENCE MAKERS."
- CLAY CLARK

WE HELP YOU TO IMPLEMENT THE FOLLOWING CLAY CLARK SUCCESS STRATEGIES, SYSTEMS, AND PROVEN PROCESSES (AND MORE):

- Graphic Designers
- Web Designers
- Save Years of Trial & Error
- Search Engine Optimization
- Management/Leadership Training
- Online Advertisement
- Public Relations
- Speaking Coaching
- Sales Training
- Billing Systems Creation
- Brand Enhancement
- Website Creation
- Proven Systems for Massive Growth
- Installation of New Employee Recruitment Systems & Processes
- Bookkeeping/Accounting Systems Creation
- Sales Scripting Installation
- Dream 100 System Creation
- Online Advertisement Design & Creation
- On-Going Group Interview / Employee Hiring, Inspiring, Training and Retaining Systems
- On-Going Sales Management
- On-Going Sales Training
- On-Going Management Training
- Workflow Design
- On-Going Advertisement Management
- On-Going Dream 100 Marketing
- On-Going Lead Tracking
- On-Going Online Reputation Management
- On-Going Search Engine Optimization
- Print Piece Design

WINDOW NINJAS.

Gabriel Salinas
Owner / Founder
www.WindowNinjas.com/

WILL **YOU** BE THE **NEXT SUCCESS STORY?**

Schedule your free consultation with Clay Clark today!
www.thrivetimeshow.com

CHAPTER 06

TIME-SENSITIVE

Time is the most important asset we have on the planet Earth. We can always make more money, but we can't make more time. Our lives are not a dress rehearsal, and the sooner that we can begin to turn our dreams into reality with a sense of urgency, the better. Having worked with thousands of business owners over the past 20 years, I have discovered that ONLY THAT WHICH GETS SCHEDULED GETS DONE.

For example, I am typing out and writing this specific chapter of this book at 4:47 p.m. in Scotland. This is not by accident. I am writing this specific chapter of this specific book at this specific time because I scheduled it. I blocked out time to write this chapter of the book, and I blocked out this afternoon to tour Glasgow, Scotland. In your business and in life, nothing will get done unless it is scheduled. Having a proven mentor and coaching program will push you to block out time to work on your business and not just passively drift in "busyness."

NOTABLE QUOTABLE

"In order to help to set TIME SENSITIVE goals that you will actually achieve, I would encourage you to invest 90 seconds to answer the following questions about yourself and your fitness goals- What is your actual body weight? What is your SPECIFIC and ideal goal body weight? Why do you ideally want to be at your goal body weight? How would you actually feel about yourself if you achieved your body weight goals? At this exact moment in time, how do you feel about your body weight and your body shape?

If you do not set any TIME SENSITIVE goals related to your fitness and health and you stay on your current course, where will your health and weight be in 1 year from now? Why do you eat what you eat? Why do you eat when you eat? Why do you currently work out as much or as little as you currently do?

You must be intentional to design the life that you want to live, and in order to do this, you must become a MASTER at setting TIME SENSITIVE goals and I am here to help great people like you to do just that!"

- COLTON CLAUSSEN
(The Founder of www.ClaussenTulsaPersonalTraining.com)

NOTABLE QUOTABLE

"Your destiny is not a matter of luck, it is the result of the choices you make on a daily basis. These choices will either elevate you or cause your dreams to sink. Decide today to be everything you have been created to be and everything you deserve. Your success is in your hands."

- SHARON LECHTER

(Sharon Lechter is a multiple-time www.ThrivetimeShow.com Podcast guest, the co-author of Rich Dad Poor Dad, a CPA, and a legendary entrepreneur and best-selling author.)

As an example of an entrepreneur that is now thriving, we have had the pleasure to help a Canadian-based accountant by the name of Josh Spurrell to systemize, grow, and scale his accounting practice (which you can learn more about at: www. Spurrell.CA). Every week when working together, I noticed that Josh always had great follow through on the action items and deadlines. As an accountant, he already had a full schedule that was filled with helping his clients with their finances, taxes, investments, and their overall financial planning. So where did he find the time to proactively grow and scale his business? Josh was a master manager of time, and he instinctively understood the need to block out a significant amount of time to grow his business. He understood that growing, systemizing, and scaling his business was a TIME SENSITIVE endeavor.

As a result, over the past 6+ years, we have worked together, Josh has since grown his accounting practice tremendously, and even internationally. He has always been coachable, diligent, and he consistently chose to take action on the TIME SENSITIVE aspects of growing a business.

NOTABLE QUOTABLE

"Do not wait: the time will never be 'just right'. Start where you stand, and work whatever tools you may have at your command and better tools will be found as you go along."

- NAPOLEON HILL

(The best-selling author of Think & Grow Rich which is the best-selling self-help book of all time. The book that forever changed my life, which is why I named my son Aubrey Napoleon-Hill Clark.)

"So we went from $3 million in revenue with 3 offices. Now we have 17 offices across 4 states. Last year we did $20 million. We are 7X larger! Clay Clark has magnified the reach we have. It's allowed us to be more selective. We brought in 400 inbound clients this month. It magnified the reach we have. These clients are calling us! You give practical steps on what to do. Clay, you taught me there is a pattern to success. You clearly define the success pattern. Clay you are the guy that takes away excuses.'

- PAUL HOOD
(CPA and Founder of www.HoodCPAs.com)

FOCUS. SACRFICE. WIN

'ONE OF THE PENALTIES OF LEADERSHIP IS THE NECESSITY OF WILLINGNESS UPON THE PART OF THE LEADER TO DO MORE THAN HE REQUIRES OF HIS FOLLOWERS.'
- NAPOLEON HILL
FAMED SUCCESS AUTHOR

How long does it take to grow a successful business? It really comes down to the business owner's choice to work with a sense of urgency and to take the action steps that need to be done. Over the past 20 years, I have helped thousands of entrepreneurs to completely transform their lives and businesses by following the proven path outlined below. But it is up to YOU as the entrepreneur to work with a sense of urgency, to block out the time needed to grow your business, and to embrace the TIME SENSITIVE nature and SENSE OF URGENCY REQUIRED to grow a successful business.

> Step 1 - Establish Your Revenue Goals

> Step 2 - Determine Your Break-Even Numbers

> Step 3 - Define the Number of Hours Per Week You Are Willing to Work

> Step 4 - Define Your Unique Value Proposition

> Step 5 - Improve Branding

> Step 6 - Create 3-Legged Marketing Stool & a Powerful No-Brainer

> Step 7 - Create a Sales Conversion System

> Step 8 - Determine Sustainable Customer Acquisition Costs

> Step 9 - Create Repeatable Systems, Processes & File Organization

> Step 10 - Create Management Execution Systems

> Step 11 - Create a Sustainable & Repetitive Weekly Schedule

> Step 12 - Create Human Resources & Recruitment Systems

> Step 13 - Create Accounting & Automate Earning Millions

> Step 14 - Determine the Point of Achieving Financial Success

Owning a business is like having a gym membership; you can get as much or as little out of your business as you want to.

It's entirely possible to have a gym membership, never use it, and never actually get into shape. Fitness owners agree-the gym members who take the initiative to schedule or pre-schedule their recurring workouts are the ones that get into the best physical shape. Why? All gym members have access to the same fitness equipment, so why do the members that have a pre-scheduled workout time have the best results? Much like hiring a proven mentor or business coaching program to help you grow your business, a fitness trainer provides you with the TOOLS needed to be successful. the ACCOUNTABILITY needed to get the work done, and the MOTIVATION needed to stay engaged throughout the process. As a business coach, I cannot emphasize enough how important it is to set aside specific time to work on the action steps and growth of your business.

NOTABLE QUOTABLE

"Most people are sitting on their own diamond mines. The surest ways to lose your diamond mine are to get bored, become overambitious, or start thinking that the grass is greener on the other side. Find your core focus, stick to it, and devote your time and resources to excelling at it."

- GINO WICKMAN

(The legendary business consultant, best-selling author of Traction: Get a Grip on Your Business and a multiple-time ThrivetimeShow.com Podcast guest.)

NOTABLE QUOTABLE

"Your reputation is what people believe you to be; your character is what you really are. Build your character strongly, and your reputation can look out for itself."

- NAPOLEON HILL

(The life-changing and best-selling author of Think & Grow Rich. Clay Clark named his son Aubrey Napoleon-Hill Clark after Napoleon Hill.)

NOTABLE QUOTABLE

"Preparation is everything."

- DAVID ROBINSON

(A multiple-time www.ThrivetimeShow.com Podcast guest, a retired NBA great who played for the San Antonio Spurs in the National Basketball Association (NBA) from 1989 to 2003. David is a minority owner of the Spurs. David was nicknamed "the Admiral" for his time spent in the U.S. Navy. Robinson was a 10-time NBA All-Star, the 1995 NBA MVP, a two-time NBA champion (1999 and 2003), a two-time Olympic Gold Medal winner (1992, 1996), a two-time Naismith Memorial Basketball Hall of Fame inductee (2009 for his individual career, 2010 as a member of the 1992 United States men's Olympic basketball team), and a two-time U.S. Olympic Hall of Fame inductee (2008 individually, 2009 as a member of the 1992 Olympic team). He was honored as one of the league's all-time players by being named to the NBA 50th Anniversary (1996) and 75th Anniversary Teams (2021). He is widely considered one of the greatest centers in both college basketball and NBA history.)

NOTABLE QUOTABLE

"With no clear picture of how you wish your life to be, how on earth are you going to live it? What is your Primary Aim? Where is the script to make your dreams come true? What is the first step to take and how do you measure your progress? How far have you gone and how close are you to getting to your goals?"

- MICHAEL GERBER

(The renowned business consultant, ThrivetimeShow.com Podcast guest, and best-selling author of the The E-myth book series.)

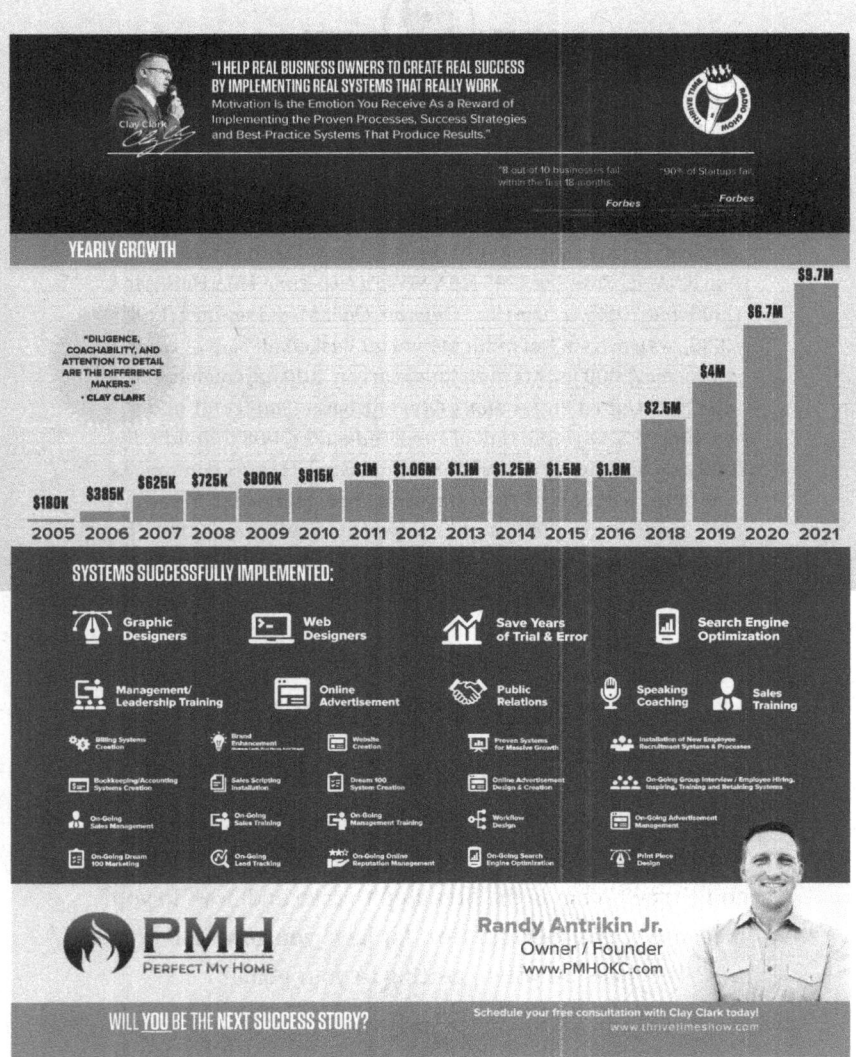

CHAPTER 07

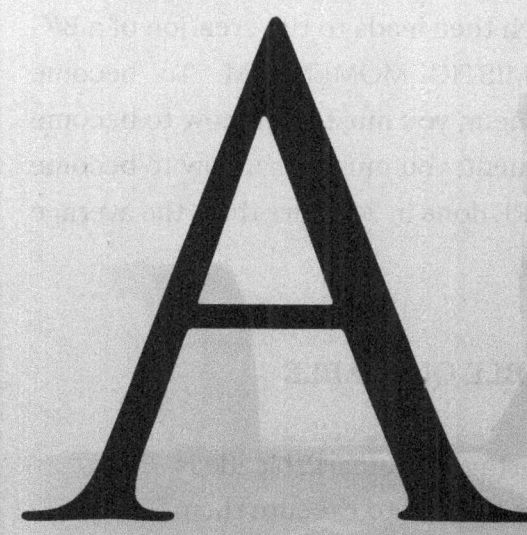

ACTION
FOCUSED

NOTABLE QUOTABLE

"Success seems to be connected with action.
Successful people keep moving. They make
mistakes, but they don't quit."

- CONRAD HILTON

*(A man who we never interviewed on the www.ThrivetimeShow.com Podcast
because he was dead before I was born in 1980. Conrad Nicholson Hilton
(December 25, 1887 – January 3, 1979) was an American hotel magnate and
politician who founded the Hilton Hotels chain. From 1912 to 1916, Hilton was
a Republican representative in the first New Mexico Legislature, but became
disillusioned with the "inside deals" of politics. In 1919, he purchased his first
hotel, the Mobley Hotel in Cisco, Texas, for $40 000 (equivalent to $725,451
in 2024) and subsequently capitalized on the oil boom. The rooms were
rented out in eight-hour shifts. He continued to purchase and sell hotels, and
eventually established the world's first international hotel chain. When he
died in 1979, he left the bulk of his estate to the Conrad N. Hilton Foundation.)*

Success is achieved by taking the ACTION that will help you gain TRACTION, which then leads to the creation of a BIG OVERWHELMING OPTIMISTIC MOMENTUM. To become successful as an entrepreneur, you must learn how to become a master of time management; you must learn how to become a person who can get MORE done in 24 hours than the average man or woman.

NOTABLE QUOTABLE

"There's no shortage of remarkable ideas, what's missing is the will to execute them."

- SETH GODIN
(A www.ThrivetimeShow.com Podcast guest, New York Times Best-Selling Author of Purple Cow, and former Yahoo! Vice President of Marketing.)

Having taught thousands and thousands of entrepreneurs at our in-person 2-day interactive www.ThrivetimeShow.com business conferences, I am always most excited to learn about how the entrepreneurs are able to implement what they are learning once they return to their local businesses. Oftentimes when I follow up with conference attendees, I am told that their biggest challenge in route to achieving success is getting their team, their employees, and those around them to diligently implement the proven processes and best-practice success systems that they learned.

NOTABLE QUOTABLE

"Before success comes in any man's life, he's sure to meet with much temporary defeat and, perhaps, some failures. When defeat overtakes a man, the easiest and the most logical thing to do is to quit. That's exactly what the majority of men do."

- NAPOLEON HILL

(The legendary author of the best-selling self-help book of all-time, Think & Grow Rich. I named my son Aubrey Napoleon-Hill Clark because Napoleon Hill's book Think & Grow Rich changed my life.)

As an example, years ago, I was asked to speak on several occasions to a wonderful group of appliance store owners as part of Maytag University. At these in-person workshops, we were tirelessly and passionately teaching the proven systems that would allow the local business owners to DRAMATICALLY INCREASE their profitability. Because I was asked to speak at multiple events, I had an opportunity to follow up with the local owners and to track their success.

What I found was that the owners who were the most ACTION FOCUSED and focused on implementation of what they had learned were the ones who achieved the most success. Furthermore, I discovered that the local owners who were having the most success were the ones who were implementing one form of merit-based pay or another as a way to get their team to take massive action. This way, they incentivized the employees who were taking the right action and penalized the employees who refused to implement the new systems and processes.

Dave, who attended the Maytag workshop, called me after I spoke. He said, "Clay, I love what you taught at Maytag University, but I am getting almost 0% buy-in from my team. I would like to hire you to coach me and to help me implement the systems you taught. I did the math. Even if you only help me to grow by 5%, it will pay for the $1,700 per month I am paying you. So let's do it!"

NOTABLE QUOTABLE

"Today I will do what others won't, so tomorrow I will do what others can't."

- JERRY RICE

(Jerry Lee Rice is an American former professional football wide receiver who played for 20 seasons in the National Football League (NFL). He won three Super Bowl titles with the San Francisco 49ers before playing two shorter stints at the end of his career with the Oakland Raiders and Seattle Seahawks.)

NOTABLE QUOTABLE

"When my clients come to train with me, they are coming because they want to take MASSIVE ACTION towards their goals. My clients view every workout with me as another step closer to the achievement of their goals. As a personal trainer, my entire career is focussed on helping people to take MASSIVE ACTION to improve their health, physique and overall well-being. At the end of the day, you can read every book there is to read about fitness, but until you begin to physically move your body and change your diet, nothing will change."

- COLTON CLAUSSEN

(The Founder of www.ClaussenTulsaPersonalTraining.com)

NOTABLE QUOTABLE

"Acta Non Verba. Watch what a person does and not what a person says."

- ROBERT KIYOSAKI

(The legendary best-selling author of the Rich Dad Poor Dad book series, an prolific investor, a legendary podcast, a life-long entrepreneurship educator, the co-author of two books with President Donald J. Trump, a multiple-time www. ThrivetimeShow.com podcast guest and www.ThrivetimeShow. com Business Conference presenter.)

I scheduled a FREE 13-point assessment with Dave so that I could determine the best way to help him implement the systems below:

> Step 1 - Establish Your Revenue Goals

> Step 2 - Determine Your Break-Even Numbers

> Step 3 - Define the Number of Hours Per Week You Are Willing to Work

> Step 4 - Define Your Unique Value Proposition

> Step 5 - Improve Branding

> Step 6 - Create 3-Legged Marketing Stool & a Powerful No-Brainer

> Step 7 - Create a Sales Conversion System

> Step 8 - Determine Sustainable Customer Acquisition Costs

> Step 9 - Create Repeatable Systems, Processes & File Organization

> Step 10 - Create Management Execution Systems

> Step 11 - Create a Sustainable & Repetitive Weekly Schedule

> Step 12 - Create Human Resources & Recruitment Systems

> Step 13 - Create Accounting & Automate Earning Millions

> Step 14 - Determine the Point of Achieving Financial Success

NOTABLE QUOTABLE

"Most leaders know that bringing discipline and accountability to the organization will make people a little uncomfortable. That's an inevitable part of creating traction. What usually holds an organization back is the fear of creating this discomfort."

- GINO WICKMAN

(A multiple-time www.ThrivetimeShow.com Podcast guest, a best-selling author and entrepreneur educator.)

After conducting the FREE 13-point assessment with Dave, I knew that I could help him DOUBLE the size of his business in 12 months or less. In order to do this, we needed to knock out the following items IMMEDIATELY-

> STEP 1 - Install a Tracking Sheet

> STEP 2 - Implement the sights, sounds, smells, tastes, and experiences in-store checklist

> STEP 3 - Optimize His Local Website

> STEP 4 - Optimize His Online Reputation

> STEP 5 - Call All Former Customers & Invite Them In to Experience His Updated Showroom & His Appliance Specials & Discounts

> STEP 6 - Implement an Intentional Show Room Experience That Is Focused On Using a Daily Checklist to Enhance the Sights, Sounds, Smells, Customer Experience, Phone Greeting, & In-Store Greeting

> STEP 7 - Implement a Turn-Key Hiring Process for Hiring, Inspiring, Training, and Retaining Employees So That Dave Could Never Be Held Hostage By Poor Performing Employees Again

> STEP 8 - Install the Attention and Traffic Generating Exterior Signage

NOTABLE QUOTABLE

"First comes thought; then organization of that thought, into ideas and plans; then transformation of those plans into reality. The beginning, as you will observe, is in your imagination."

- NAPOLEON HILL

(The best-selling self-help author of all-time whose writings changed my life and the man whom I chose to name my son Aubrey Napoleon-Hill Clark after.)

As I met with Dave each week, I found out that the biggest issue he was facing was that his employees were outright refusing to implement any of the new processes and business growing systems. With my guidance, I helped Dave overcome this challenge by implementing a merit-based pay system. Employees would earn money based on the work they actually accomplished, and if an employee refused to do the work or implement the new system, it would negatively affect their paychecks. Whether this is a negative observation or a positive observation, I have found that most employees do not care about implementing action items correctly until they discover how it will positively or negatively impact their paychecks and their wallets. I have found that you can give a thousand talks to your team about the importance of following daily systems and processes, but until it impacts your employees financially, most employees don't care and won't care.

NOTABLE QUOTABLE

"I travel probably four days a week. That's the game of international development. You have to be at your properties. No developer is successful sitting behind their desk."

- ERIC TRUMP

(The multiple-time www.ThrivetimeShow.com Podcast guest, a multiple-time www.ThrivetimeShow.com Conference speaker, a friend of mine, the son of President Donald J. Trump and the man who runs the entire Trump Organization which consists of 5,000+ employees and billions of dollars of assets as a trustee and executive vice president of the Trump Organization.)

To Dave's credit, he had become sick and tired of begging his employees to change, so he was 100% bought into the new method. Without hesitation, Dave implemented merit-based pay and the concept of providing incentives for great performance and penalties for poor performance. Because of this one change in his business, we were able to implement growth at a rapid rate. This allowed him to nearly DOUBLE the performance of his store in just under 12 MONTHS.

NOTABLE QUOTABLE

"Your beliefs become your thoughts. Your thoughts become your words. Your words become your actions. Your actions become your habits. Your habits become your values. Your values become your destiny."

- GANDHI

(Mohandas Karamchand Gandhi, (October 2, 1869 – January 30, 1948) was an Indian lawyer, anti-colonial nationalist, and political ethicist who employed nonviolent resistance to lead the successful campaign for India's independence from British rule. He inspired movements for civil rights and freedom across the world. The honorific Mahātmā (from Sanskrit, meaning great-souled, or venerable), first applied to him in South Africa in 1914, is now used throughout the world.)

Dave recognized that in order for his results to change, he had to create an organization that was ACTION FOCUSED. Dave recognized that merely learning success systems at a workshop wasn't enough. He knew he had to change the ACTIONS that he and his team were taking on a daily basis. This might seem obvious, but you would be shocked how few business owners take the step to stop talking and to start implementing proven systems. A proven mentor and business coaching program will take massive action with BIG OVERWHELMING OPTIMISTIC MOMENTUM. Growing a real business is very different from watching a TedTalks video or attending a theoretical college course filled with ultra-deep and academic business jargon. Growing a business requires being ACTION FOCUSED.

NOTABLE QUOTABLE

"The way to get started is to quit talking
and begin doing."

- WALT DISNEY

*(Walter Elias Disney, (December 5, 1901 – December 15, 1966)
was an American animator, film producer, voice actor, and
entrepreneur. A pioneer of the American animation industry, he
introduced several developments in the production of cartoons.
As a film producer, he holds the record for most Academy Awards
earned (22) and nominations (59) by an individual. He was
presented with two Golden Globe Special Achievement Awards
and an Emmy Award, among other honors. Several of his films
are included in the National Film Registry by the Library of
Congress and have also been named as some of the greatest films
ever by the American Film Institute.)*

NOTABLE QUOTABLE

"Success is neither magical nor mysterious. Success is
the natural consequence of consistently applying the
basic fundamentals."

- JIM ROHN

*(Jim was an American entrepreneur, author, and motivational
speaker. He wrote numerous books including, How to Obtain
Wealth and Happiness. Rohn mentored Mark R. Hughes and life
strategist Tony Robbins in the late 1970s. Others who credit Rohn
for influencing their careers include authors/lecturers Mark
Victor Hansen and Jack Canfield (Chicken Soup book series),
Everton Edwards (Hallmark Innovators Conglomerate), Brian
Tracy, Darren Hardy, and Harv Eker. Rohn coauthored the novel
Twelve Pillars with Chris Widener.)*

OPPORTUNITY

NOTE: *This was my grandfather Ben Meinhardt's favorite poem. My grandfather was a successful entrepreneur, skilled electrician and loving father / grandfather.)*

"THIS I beheld, or dreamed it in a dream:--

There spread a cloud of dust along a plain;

And underneath the cloud, or in it, raged

A furious battle, and men yelled, and swords

Shocked upon swords and shields. A prince's banner

Wavered, then staggered backward, hemmed by foes.

A craven hung along the battle's edge,

And thought, "Had I a sword of keener steel--

That blue blade that the king's son bears, -- but this

Blunt thing--!" he snapped and flung it from his hand,

And lowering crept away and left the field.

Then came the king's son, wounded, sore bestead,

And weaponless, and saw the broken sword,

Hilt-buried in the dry and trodden sand,

And ran and snatched it, and with battle shout

Lifted afresh he hewed his enemy down,

And saved a great cause that heroic day."

EDWARD ROWLAND SILL (1841-1887)

"I HELP REAL BUSINESS OWNERS TO CREATE REAL SUCCESS BY IMPLEMENTING REAL SYSTEMS THAT REALLY WORK. Motivation Is the Emotion You Receive As a Reward of Implementing the Proven Processes, Success Strategies and Best-Practice Systems That Produce Results."

Clay Clark

"8 out of 10 businesses fail within the first 18 months.
Forbes

"96% of Startups fail.
Forbes

YEAR TO DATE REVENUE PROGRESS:

Year	Revenue
2015	$24,137,419
2016	$40,469,152
2017	$48,458,317
2018	$50,976,592
2019	$64,443,539
2020	$132,041,046

"DILIGENCE, COACHABILITY, AND ATTENTION TO DETAIL ARE THE DIFFERENCE MAKERS."
- CLAY CLARK

WE HELP YOU TO IMPLEMENT THE FOLLOWING CLAY CLARK SUCCESS STRATEGIES, SYSTEMS, AND PROVEN PROCESSES (AND MORE):

- Graphic Designers
- Web Designers
- Save Years of Trial & Error
- Search Engine Optimization
- Management/ Leadership Training
- Online Advertisement
- Public Relations
- Speaking Coaching
- Sales Training
- Billing Systems Creation
- Brand Enhancement
- Website Creation
- Proven Systems for Massive Growth
- Installation of New Employee Recruitment Systems & Processes
- Bookkeeping/Accounting Systems Creation
- Sales Scripting Installation
- Dream 100 System Creation
- Online Advertisement Design & Creation
- On-Going Group Interview / Employee Hiring, Implenting, Training and Retaining Systems
- On-Going Sales Management
- On-Going Sales Training
- On-Going Management Training
- Workflow Design
- On-Going Advertisement Management
- On-Going Dream 100 Marketing
- On-Going Lead Tracking
- On-Going Online Reputation Management
- On-Going Search Engine Optimization
- Print Place Design

SHAW HOMES

Glen Shaw & Aaron Antis
Shaw Homes
www.ShawHomes.com

WILL **YOU** BE THE NEXT SUCCESS STORY?

Schedule your free consultation with Clay Clark today!
www.thrivetimeshow.com

CHAPTER 08

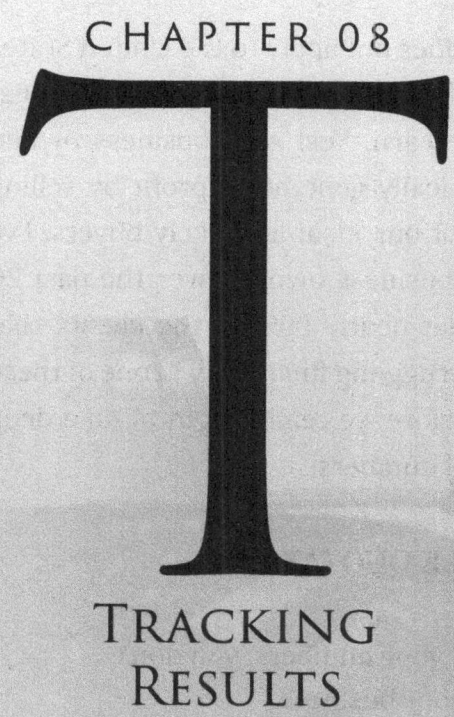

T
Tracking Results

NOTABLE QUOTABLE

"Don't ever let your business get ahead of the financial side of your business. Accounting, accounting, accounting. Know your numbers."

- TILMAN FERTITTA

(Tilman Joseph Fertitta is an American businessman and television personality. He has served as the United States ambassador to Italy and San Marino since May 2025. He is owner of Landry's, Inc. He also owns the National Basketball Association (NBA)'s Houston Rockets. Fertitta has been the chairman of the board of regents of the University of Houston System since 2009. Tilman Fertitta earned his riches through a combination of business ventures and timely wise business acquisitions, particularly in the hospitality and restaurant industries. He started with construction and development, eventually focusing on acquiring and growing restaurant chains under the Landry's Inc. umbrella. He also expanded into casinos and sports, owning the Houston Rockets.)

Although this principle does not apply to the United States government and bureaucrats who work for it, you and I must spend less money than we earn. Yes! As a business owner, you and I must unapologetically generate a profit by selling solutions to the problems of our ideal and likely buyers. I've worked with thousands of business owners over the past 20 years and I can tell you that nearly 99% of the clients that work with us are typically struggling financially in one of these following 5 areas, that is, before we really begin to do a deep dive look into their financial numbers.

NOTABLE QUOTABLE

"If you don't know your numbers, you don't know your business."

- MARCUS LEMONIS

(Marcus Anthony Lemonis is a Lebanese-American businessman, TV personality, and philanthropist. He serves as the chairman and CEO of Camping World, Good Sam Enterprises, and Beyond. Additionally, he is renowned for his role as the star of The Profit, a CNBC reality show about saving small businesses.)

1st - Acting Like a Bank When You And Your Business Are Not a Bank - Most well intentioned clients will unintentionally or intentionally extend financing terms to clients that no bank in America could offer to customers. For example- contractors will buy the supplies upfront, will front the costs of all of the labor associated with the work being done, send the customer an invoice 15 days later, and then give the customers another 30 days or more to pay the bill. This, my friend, will cause death by invoice.

NOTABLE QUOTABLE

"It's not how much money you make. It's how much money you keep"

- ROBERT KIYOSAKI

(A multiple-time www.ThrivetimeShow.com Podcast guest, a www.ThrivetimeShow.com Business Conference Speaker, the author of the best-selling Rich Dad Poor Dad book series, an investor, a podcaster and financial educator.)

2nd - Employing a Large Team of People That Do Not Receive Merit-Based & Results-Based Pay - Employees don't complete jobs, yet they still get paid. Employees are often assigned to do nothing and held accountable for doing nothing, yet they still get paid. I often find managers that don't manage, social media coordinators that don't coordinate social media, bookkeepers that don't keep the books, marketing managers that don't manage, and so on. Employees don't do their jobs, and yet they are still getting paid. Meanwhile, you as the owner are financially struggling. You must create a culture where everyone on your team gets paid when your business gets paid, and a culture where your employees get paid for the work they DO, not for the work they INTEND on doing.

NOTABLE QUOTABLE

"Review your goals twice every day in order to be focused on achieving them."

- LES BROWN
(The legendary motivational speaker, best-selling author and self-help guru.)

3rd - Employees Are Using Your Business Like Their Personal Credit Card to Buy Things That They Want That Are Entirely Not Related to the Business - As a business owner, you simply cannot allow most people within your organization to buy items and services without there being some intense levels of accountability in place. WASTE AND FRAUD are always two of the biggest sources of expense that I find when I work with business owners to help them get on top of their businesses finances . As a business owner, you simply cannot pass out company credit cards to teammates. You cannot expect employees who are dysfunctional in their own personal financial lives to suddenly become financially disciplined when using your company's finances.

4th - Perpetually Buying Items That Are Not Used - In the world we now live in, it is very easy to endlessly buy, autoship, or subscribe to purchasing products and services on a monthly basis that you and your business do not really need. As a business owner, every expense that your business undergoes should be related to the business, to growing the business, and to making the business better. A proven business mentor or business coaching program will be willing to look at your finances on a weekly or monthly basis to make sure that you don't have runaway, wasteful spending growing within your business.

NOTABLE QUOTABLE

"Accounting numbers, of course, are the language of business and as such are of enormous help to anyone evaluating the worth of a business and tracking its progress. Charlie and I would be lost without these numbers; they invariably are the starting point for us in evaluating our own businesses and those of others. Managers and owners need to remember, however, that accounting is but an aid to business thinking, never a substitute for it."

- WARREN BUFFETT

(Warren Edward Buffett is an American investor and philanthropist who currently serves as the chairman and CEO of the conglomerate holding company Berkshire Hathaway. As a result of his investment success, Buffett is one of the best-known investors in the world. According to Forbes, as of May 2025, Buffett's estimated net worth stood at $160.2 billion, making him the fifth-richest individual in the world. Berkshire Hathaway invests in a wide range of companies across multiple industries. A few of Berkshire Hathaway's most known holdings include now Apple, American Express, Coca-Cola, Bank of America, and Chevron. Berkshire also has significant ownership in companies like Precision Castparts, Lubrizol, GEICO, McLane, and Duracell. In addition, Berkshire Hathaway has a large portfolio of wholly-owned subsidiaries, including Berkshire Hathaway Energy, Clayton Homes, Dairy Queen, and Fruit of the Loom.)

NOTABLE QUOTABLE

"Risk comes from not knowing what
you're doing"

- WARREN BUFFETT

*(Warren Buffett (Warren Edward Buffett is an American investor
and philanthropist who currently serves as the chairman and
CEO of the conglomerate holding company Berkshire Hathaway.
As a result of his investment success, Buffett is one of the best-
known investors in the world. According to Forbes, as of May 2025,
Buffett's estimated net worth stood at US$160.2 billion, making
him the fifth-richest individual in the world. Berkshire Hathaway
invests in a wide range of companies across multiple industries.
A few of Berkshire Hathaway's most known holdings include
now Apple, American Express, Coca-Cola, Bank of America, and
Chevron. Berkshire also has significant ownership in companies
like Precision Castparts, Lubrizol, GEICO, McLane, and Duracell.
In addition, Berkshire Hathaway has a large portfolio of wholly-
owned subsidiaries, including Berkshire Hathaway Energy, Clayton
Homes, Dairy Queen, and Fruit of the Loom.)*

5th - Not Looking At Your Numbers On A Weekly Basis - Delegating your Finances to a bookkeeper, an accountant, an outsourced chief financial officer, a chief financial officer, a spouse, an employee, a brother-in-law, a business partner, or anybody that is not you is not a good idea. You must know your numbers.

IT'S NOT ABOUT HOW MUCH YOU MAKE,
ITS ABOUT HOW MUCH YOU KEEP.
-CLAY CLARK

NOTABLE QUOTABLE

"A budget is telling your money where to go
instead of wondering where it went."

- DAVE RAMSEY

(The legendary best-selling author, radio talk show host,
podcaster, financial coach, entrepreneur and investor.)

Delegating your finances, your financial accountability, your financial success and your money to be watched over by anybody other than you is a form of self-hate that I cannot understand. It will cause you massive and well-deserved financial problems. Allowing another person to be responsible for your finances would be like a married man allowing another man to sleep in the same bedroom with his wife while he is on a business trip in order to keep her safe. My friend, do not self-sabotage. You must look at your finances on a weekly basis. You must measure what you treasure. You track where you don't want to slack and you must NEVER DELEGATE YOUR FINANCIAL RESPONSIBILITY TO ANYONE ELSE.

NOTABLE QUOTABLE

"Financial peace isn't the acquisition of stuff. It's learning to live on less than you make, so you can give money back and have money to invest. You can't win until you do this."

- DAVE RAMSEY
(The legendary best-selling author, radio talk show host, podcaster, financial coach, entrepreneur and investor.)

As an example of a client who stays on top of their finances, I think about Andrew Sorchini and his team at Beverly Hills Precious Metals (www.BH-PM.com). Every hour of every day, he and his team buy and sell specific amounts of gold and silver at specific prices. They then ship that product to specific people who live at specific addresses all around the world. In his business, and in every business, the DETAILS MATTER. Over the years, I have helped Andrew and his team with their marketing, their branding, and many of their sales processes, and Andrew has always been on top of his own finances.

NOTABLE QUOTABLE

"If you don't track your results, you will begin to drift with your health. If you do not track your results, you will begin to notice yourself saying yes to eating the wrong foods and yes to skipping your workouts. In business and in life, you must measure what you treasure, because by default we all slack where we don't track."

- COLTON CLAUSSEN
(The Founder of www.ClaussenTulsaPersonalTraining.com)

Another example of diligent, coachable, long-time clients who are choosing to stay on top of their finances are the folks at www.RockHavenRetrievers.com. They are very intentional about choosing to know their numbers on a consistent basis. Every hour of every day, customers go online at www.RockHavenRetrievers.com to learn about buying a dog. When a customer buys a specific dog, the good folks at www.RockHavenRetrievers.com have to send the specific dog that was ordered to the specific customer. That customer has a specific address where they want the specific dogs they ordered to be shipped. In their business, the DETAILS MATTER. Whether it is precious metals, breeding dogs, cleaning carpets, building houses, or rendering any other type of product or service to your ideal and likely buyers on the planet Earth in exchange for a profit, you have to know your numbers. You must schedule a time each and every week to go over your numbers with your proven mentor and business coaching program. If you don't have a proven mentor or a business coaching program, I simply cannot understand the self-emposed financial jackassery and financial chaos that you are choosing to experience.

> You not looking at your finances every week would be like going to the restroom and trusting that someone else would wipe your butt clean.

> You not looking at your finances on a weekly basis would be like you choosing to drive your car with a blind-fold on and trusting that your trip will be safe.

> You not looking at your finances on a weekly basis would be like you choosing to marry the first person of the opposite sex that you ever met and trusting that it will work out for the best.

> You not looking at your finances on a weekly basis would be like allowing every homeless person that you meet to live with you in your home indefinitely and trusting that it will all work out just fine.

> You not looking at your finances on a weekly basis would be like trusting that the United States Federal government will balance the budget and pay off the national debt this year.

NOTABLE QUOTABLE

"Don't ever let your business get ahead of the financial side of your business. Accounting, accounting, accounting. Know your numbers."

- TILMA FERTITTA

(Tilman Joseph Fertitta (born June 25, 1957) is an American businessman and television personality. He has served as the United States ambassador to Italy and San Marino since May 2025. He is the owner of Landry's and the National Basketball Association (NBA)'s Houston Rockets. Fertitta was the chairman of the board of regents of the University of Houston System from 2014 to 2025.)

Unless you hate yourself, you must schedule a weekly recurring time to look at the following aspects of your business-

> The total weekly income

> The total weekly expenses

> The total weekly profit

> Where your leads came from

> How much you are paying per marketing source

When you attend an in-person 2-Day Interactive www.ThrivetimeShow.com Business Growth Conference, we can do a DEEP DIVE into answering any and every business finance related question. But you CANNOT DELEGATE THE TRACKING OF YOUR FINANCES OR THE KISSING OF YOUR SPOUSE TO SOMEONE WHO IS NOT YOU UNLESS YOU WANT TO HAVE A WEIRD LIFE AND CHAOTIC LIFE.

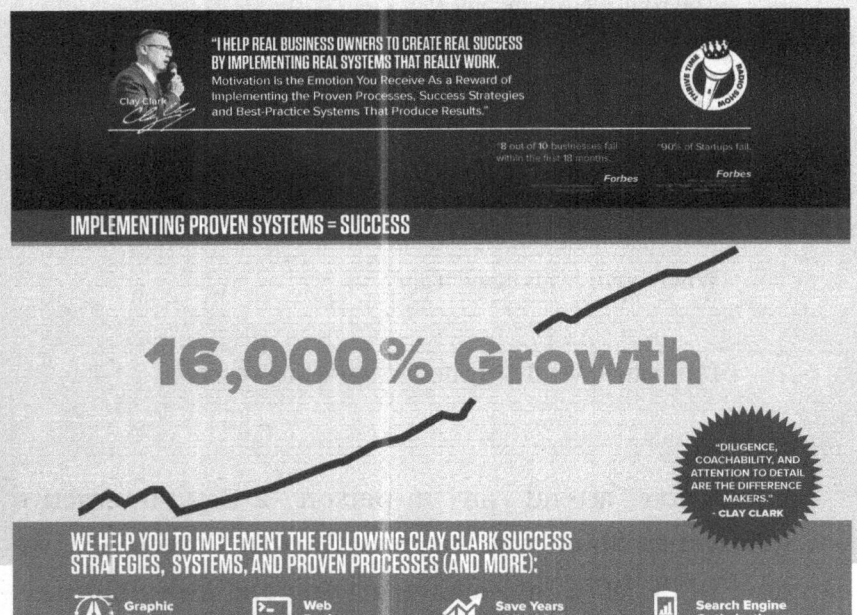

CHAPTER 09

I

ITERATING UNTIL PERFECTION

As a business consultant for 20+ years, I have found that for the most part, entrepreneurs are afraid of communicating their desire to make iterations. This is because many employees can be defensive when a business owner wants them to make changes, improvements, or enhancements to any system within their business—whether it is a checklist, system, process, marketing piece, song, movie, etc.

If you are surrounded by people who are antagonistic to the entrepreneurial rhythm and creative process of an entrepreneur, then this is not going to go well for you. You MUST create a culture where you can freely iterate without push-back from your team.

NOTABLE QUOTABLE

"Just make it exist first. You can make
it good later."

- RYAN TEDDER

*(Ryan Tedder attended Oral Roberts University in Tulsa,
Oklahoma and lived on the same college dormitory wing,
"COVENANT" with Clay Clark. Ryan Tedder worked as a waiter
at restaurants and a shop assistant at Pottery Barn before
securing an internship at DreamWorks SKG in Nashville,
Tennessee, where he sang on multiple demos. Ryan Tedder
founded OneRepublic 2002. In 2007 OneRepublic landed their
first big hit, "Apologize." Ryan Tedder has also written hits for
Beyonce, Jennifer Lopez, Jonas Brothers, Kelly Clarkson, Taylor
Swift, Tate McRae, U2, Etc.)*

The entire rhythm of entrepreneurship
should be defined as:

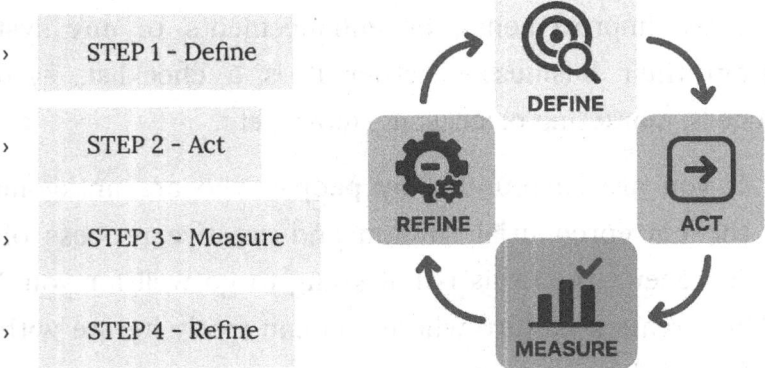

> STEP 1 - Define

> STEP 2 - Act

> STEP 3 - Measure

> STEP 4 - Refine

NOTABLE QUOTABLE

"It isn't 10,000 hours that creates outliers, it's 10,000 iterations."

- NAVAL RAVIKANT

(Naval Ravikant is an Indian-born American entrepreneur and investor. He is the co-founder, chairman and former Chief Executive Officer (CEO) of AngelList. He invested early-stage in Uber, FourSquare, Twitter, Postmates, SnapLogic, and Yammer.)

As an entrepreneur, you need to be free to DEFINE what you think is going to work. You need to ACT when you are ready to test your theories. You need to MEASURE your results to learn what is working and what is not working. Lastly, you need to endlessly REFINE or ITERATE until perfection.

"TEMPORARY FAILURES ARE A PREREQUISITE TO SUCCESS."
—NAPOLEON HILL
BEST-SELLING SUCCESS AUTHOR OF "THINK AND GROW RICH"

NOTABLE QUOTABLE

"The optimal strategy might be executing
a suboptimal plan at a fast pace. Strategy
evolves as lessons are learned—and the person
who moves faster, learns faster. Learning is a
marathon and perfection is a weighted vest."

- JAMES CLEAR
*(James Clear is an American writer. He is best known for his 2018
self-help book Atomic Habits.)*

When I think about ITERATING UNTIL PERFECTION, I think about the work we have done with www.FullPackageMedia.com, whom we have helped to grow from a startup idea into a multi-million dollar BOOMING business based in Dallas, Texas! What does the www.FullPackageMedia.com do?

When we first started working with Thomas Crosson and his start-up concept, www.FullPackageMedia.com, he needed EVERYTHING. Because it was a complete startup, Thomas needed to create everything from scratch, which is why he called us. Each week, and day by day, we created all of the systems and assets below through the process of INTERACTING UNTIL PERFECTION–

- An About Us Video
- A Booking Process
- A Call Center
- A Dream 100 Marketing / Center of Influence Marketing System
- A Hiring Process
- A Linear Workflow

- A Logo
- A Minimally Viable Product
- A New Employee On-Boarding Process
- A Pricing Model
- A Product / Service Offering
- A Proforma
- A Website
- An Organizational Chart
- Call Scripts
- Google Adwords
- Print Pieces
- Branding
- Business Cards
- Key Performance Indicators
- Metrics / Tracking Systems
- Retargeting Ads
- Search Engine Optimization
- Social Media Marketing
- Thomas Needed 100% of Everything

Starting your fitness journey and turning your goals into reality can be overwhelming if you try to climb the figurative mountain alone. However, if you commit yourself to taking small and doable daily steps while following a proven path, your success is nearly inevitable. The process involves embracing ITERATING UNTIL PERFECTION with alacrity, vivaciousness and BIG OVERWHELMING OPTIMISTIC MOMENTUM!

NOTABLE QUOTABLE

"If you can't out-iterate someone who is trying to copy you, you're toast anyway."

- ERIC RIES

(Eric Ries, born September 22, 1978, is an American entrepreneur, blogger, and author of The Lean Startup, a book on the lean startup movement. He is also the author of The Startup Way, a book on modern entrepreneurial management.)

NOTABLE QUOTABLE

"There's no shortage of remarkable ideas, what's missing is the will to execute them."

- SETH GODIN

(A www.ThrivetimeShow.com Podcast guest, New York Times Best-Selling Author of Purple Cow, and former Yahoo! Vice President of Marketing.)

Step 1 - Establish Your Revenue Goals

Step 2 - Determine Your Break-Even Numbers

Step 3 - Define the Number of Hours Per Week You Are Willing to Work

Step 4 - Define Your Unique Value Proposition

Step 5 - Improve Branding

Step 6 - Create 3-Legged Marketing Stool & a Powerful No-Brainer

Step 7 - Create a Sales Conversion System

Step 8 - Determine Sustainable Customer Acquisition Costs

Step 9 - Create Repeatable Systems, Processes & File Organization

Step 10 - Create Management Execution Systems

Step 11 - Create a Sustainable & Repetitive Weekly Schedule

Step 12 - Create Human Resources & Recruitment Systems

Step 13 - Create Accounting & Automate Earning Millions

Step 14 - Determine the Point of Achieving Financial Success

"When I coach a personal training client in the area of fitness, I simply will not let them quit. Perhaps a client cannot yet do a certain exercise, or perhaps a wonderful client has a certain physical limitation. As a trainer, I simply will not let my client quit taking care of their body, because I know that it is the only place my clients have to live. We may have to modify a movement or an exercise to accommodate a current limitation, or we may have to pivot on a nutritional plan in order to accommodate a client's dietary needs, but we are not going to quit. We are going to achieve the results."

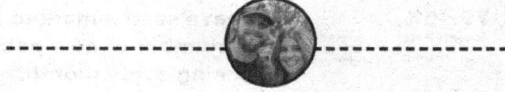

- COLTON CLAUSSEN
(The Founder of *www.ClaussenTulsaPersonalTraining.com*)

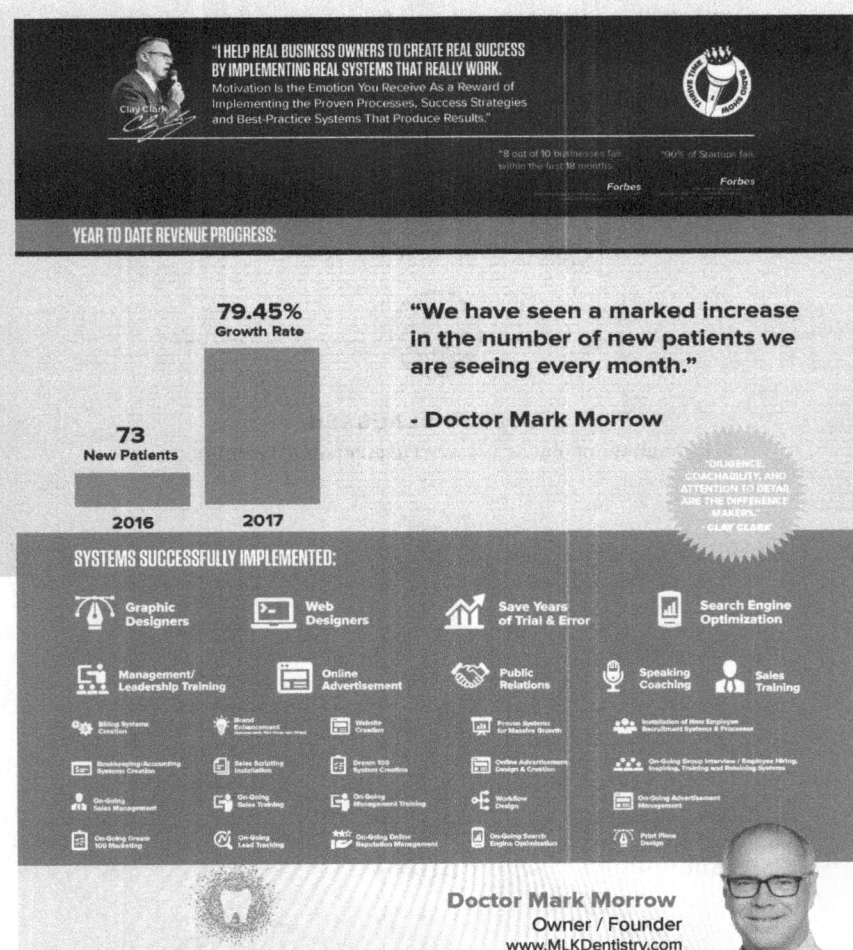

"I HELP REAL BUSINESS OWNERS TO CREATE REAL SUCCESS BY IMPLEMENTING REAL SYSTEMS THAT REALLY WORK. Motivation Is the Emotion You Receive As a Reward of Implementing the Proven Processes, Success Strategies and Best-Practice Systems That Produce Results."

Clay Clark

"8 out of 10 businesses fail within the first 18 months.
Forbes

"90% of startups fail.
Forbes

YEAR TO DATE REVENUE PROGRESS:

79.45%
Growth Rate

73
New Patients

2016   2017

"We have seen a marked increase in the number of new patients we are seeing every month."

- Doctor Mark Morrow

"DILIGENCE, COACHABILITY, AND ATTENTION TO DETAIL ARE THE DIFFERENCE MAKERS."
-CLAY CLARK

SYSTEMS SUCCESSFULLY IMPLEMENTED:

- Graphic Designers
- Web Designers
- Save Years of Trial & Error
- Search Engine Optimization
- Management/ Leadership Training
- Online Advertisement
- Public Relations
- Speaking Coaching
- Sales Training

Billing Systems Creation | Brand Enhancement | Website Creation | Proven Systems for Massive Growth | Installation of New Employee Recruitment Systems & Processes
Bookkeeping/Accounting Systems Creation | Sales Scripting Installation | Dream 100 System Creation | Online Advertisement Design & Creation | On-Going Group Interview / Employee Hiring, Inspiring, Training and Retaining Systems
On-Going Sales Management | On-Going Sales Training | On-Going Management Training | Workflow Design | On-Going Advertisement Management
On-Going Dream 100 Marketing | On-Going Lead Tracking | On-Going Online Reputation Management | On-Going Search Engine Optimization | Print Piece Design

MORROW, LAI, & KITTERMAN
PEDIATRIC DENTISTRY

Doctor Mark Morrow
Owner / Founder
www.MLKDentistry.com

WILL YOU BE THE NEXT SUCCESS STORY?

Schedule your free consultation with Clay Clark today!

CHAPTER 10

O

ON TIME & ON MISSION

Drifting aimlessly through life kills dreams. Once you set out to achieve your goals in the areas of your faith, family, finances, fitness, friends, and fun, the world around us will not stop throwing momentum-killing distractions our way. Once the motivation of setting new goals wears off, and the initial excitement of pursuing your dreams begins to be met with the reality of the daily grind, it becomes harder to stay accountable and consistent. That's why it is critical that you find a proven mentor and coaching program that will hold you accountable for being ON TIME and ON MISSION. What does that mean?

A goal is a dream with a deadline, and if we are not careful, we will not set deadlines when it comes to the achievement of our goals. The mortgage company sets a day on which you must pay your mortgage. The phone company sets a day on which you must pay your phone bill every month. But most people struggle to set hard deadlines for the achievement of their goals. This, by default, causes drifting! You must have someone in your life who holds you accountable for being ON TIME and ON MISSION when it comes to achieving your goals.

NOTABLE QUOTABLE

"Drifting, without aim or purpose, is the first cause of failure."

– NAPOLEON HILL

(The Best-selling author of Think & Grow Rich and the number one best-selling self-help author of all time.)

NOTABLE QUOTABLE

"When you are trying to get in the best shape of your life, you have to be reminded constantly to stay on MISSION. People get fat drifting in the areas of their diet and their daily physical activity. By default, most people consume too much wheat, sweets and alcohol. By default, people do not workout. As a trainer, my job is to constantly remind people to stay on mission and to make sure that day and that time is spent moving towards the achievement of their goals. We are all either moving closer to or farther away from our goals on a daily basis. This seems obvious. But everybody, including myself, must be reminded of the mission each and every day."

- COLTON CLAUSSEN

(The Founder of www.ClaussenTulsaPersonalTraining.com)

NOTABLE QUOTABLE

"People around you, constantly under the pull of their emotions, change their ideas by the day or by the hour, depending on their mood. You must never assume that what people say or do in a particular moment is a statement of their permanent desires."

- ROBERT GREENE
(A www.ThrivetimeShow.com Podcast guest and the author of the New York Times bestsellers The 48 Laws of Power, The Art of Seduction, The 33 Strategies of War, The 50th Law, Mastery, and The Laws of Human Nature.)

As an example, years ago a Certified Public Accountant by the name of Paul Hood was referred to me by a long-time client and friend in the mortgage business, Steve Currington of www.SteveCurrington.com. Before I met Paul, he had already built a nice accounting practice based in Bartlesville, Oklahoma. Although Paul was an ambitious, educated, and hardworking man, he knew that he needed a business mentor and program coaching to help him turn his dreams into reality. That is exactly why Paul decided to become a coaching client.

When we first started working with Paul at www.HoodCPAs. com, I knew immediately that he needed to change his entire branding. I suggested their brand relate to the idea of "Taking a Look Under Your Financial Hood". I showed Paul Hood how we could teach his clients to view their accounting through the windshield of their life and business, not through the rear view mirror. After multiple meetings with Paul, I became even more convinced that this was the approach that we needed to take-

> I helped Paul to create an entirely new brand for his accounting practice.

> I helped Paul to generate 40 times more inbound leads from potential accounting clients than he was previously generating by default before meeting us.

> I helped Paul to grow his accounting practice 8 times larger.

> I helped Paul to write / co-author two books.

> I helped Paul to completely renovate and redesign his physical offices to incorporate the new brand, the new marketing, and the new proactive approach to accounting that he was offering his clients.

> I helped Paul to gain the financial resources for him to build / buy a 20,000 + square dream home.

> I helped Paul to create engaging workshops for his financial planning clients to attend and learn.

How did we help Paul Hood to turn his dreams into reality? Every single week, Paul and I were ON TIME and ON MISSION; we would break the big ideas down into small, doable steps. We created steps that were Specific, Measurable, Actionable, Realistic, and Time Sensitive.

Over the next 5+ years, we helped Paul and his brand www.HoodCPAs.com to achieve 6X growth. We QUICKLY and AGGRESSIVELY guided Paul down the proven path, and the results were nothing short of EPIC. Instead of just wanting to revamp the brand, we DID revamp the brand. Instead of just wanting to write books, we DID write the books. Instead of just wanting to achieve his dreams, we actually DID help Paul Hood to achieve his dreams.

"DON'T LET SCHOOLING INTERFERE WITH YOUR EDUCATION."
– MARK TWAIN

"We have grown 15 times. Clay Clark's business coaching has been LIFE-CHANGING! There are some days now where the leads won't stop coming in. Whereas before I started working with you, I may have received 2 online leads in the previous 2-3 years. Everything had always been manual leads. Before I started working with Clay Clark I was trying to market everything manually through Instagram, but you gave me those 7 action items that I needed to do every single week. It really started to change the way the business was viewed by people around the community."

- PLACID AJOKU
(Founder of BuiltPhoenixStrong.org)

CHAPTER 11

NEVER-QUIT MENTALITY

By default, most people quit before achieving their goals. By default, most people quit reading the book before finishing it. By default, most people quit growing a business before achieving success. By default, most people set fitness goals and stop before achieving them. Why do most people quit? They quit because, by default, most people have developed the bad habit of DRIFTING. This is why we need to be intentional; we need to have a proven mentor or coaching program who pushes us and holds us accountable to a NEVER-QUIT MENTALITY.

The never-quit mentality exists in the world around us, but it is rare to find. That is why I sincerely believe that you need a coach to push you to do your best, to hold you accountable, and to never allow you to settle for anything less than your best.

NOTABLE QUOTABLE

"Nothing works unless you do."

- MAYA ANGELOU

(The critically acclaimed singer, poet and the author of several New York Times best-selling publications who was asked to share one of her poems at the inauguration for President Bill Clinton on January 20th 1993.)

NOTABLE QUOTABLE

"Your big opportunity may be right where you are now."

- NAPOLEON HILL

(Best-selling self-help author of all-time and the personal apprentice of the late great Andrew Carnegie.)

You must infuse your life with a NEVER-QUIT MENTALITY. Even your friends and family members, the most loving and caring people around you, will consciously or subconsciously push you to seek comfort and to quit instead of achieving your goals. You must not allow this to happen. Your life is way TOO IMPORTANT to waste by passively drifting along, setting goals that you never achieve.

Turn this page sideways to view this beautiful cartoon or turn your beautiful head sideways to view this beautiful cartoon.

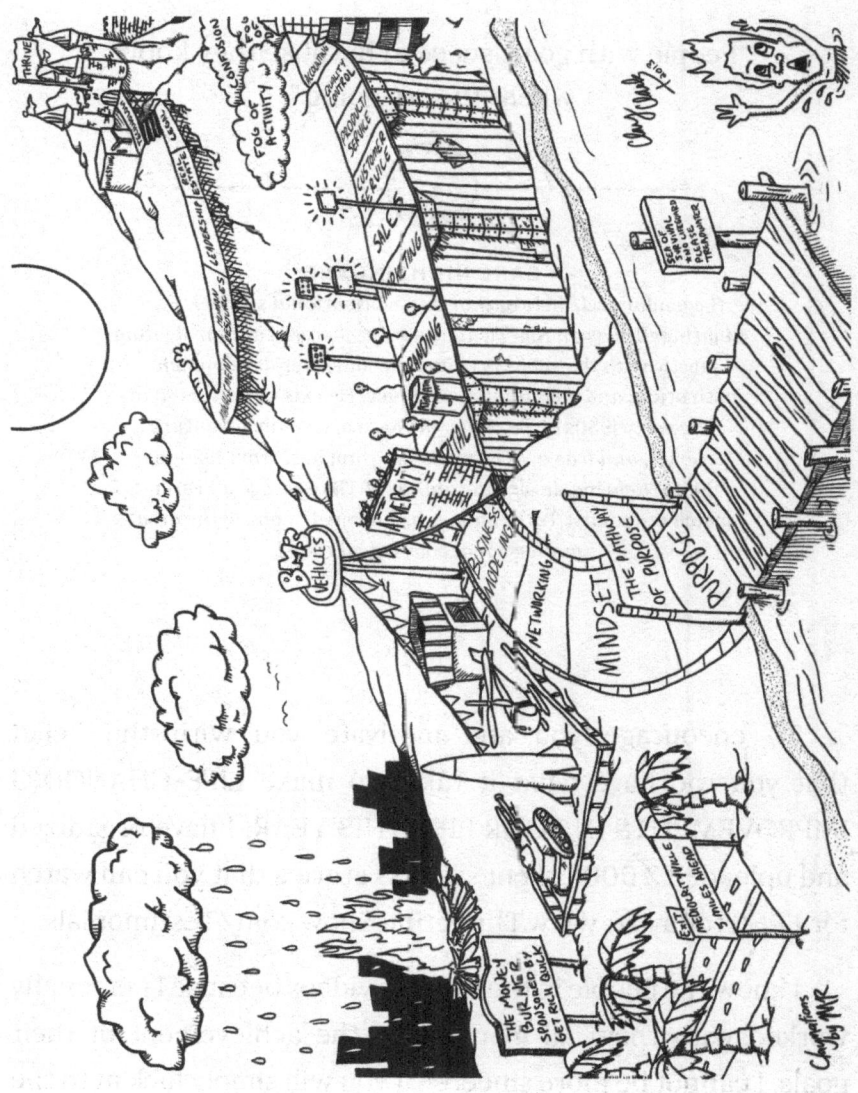

In order to help you to achieve your goals and to help you develop the HABIT of achieving massive success on a daily basis, I have included a 45 page daily success journal for you to log your daily non-negotiables and your progress.

NOTABLE QUOTABLE

"People with goals succeed because they know where they're going."

- EARL NIGHTINGALE

(Legendary self-help author and motivational speaker. Earl Nightingale was an American radio speaker and author, dealing mostly with the subjects of human character development, motivation, and meaningful existence. He was the voice during the early 1950s of Sky King, the hero of a radio adventure series, and was a WGN radio program host from 1950 to 1956. Nightingale was the author of The Strangest Secret, which economist Terry Savage has termed "...one of the great motivational books of all time.)

To encourage you and motivate you with the belief that you too have what it takes to make LIFE-CHANGING IMPROVEMENTS IN YOUR LIFE THIS YEAR, I have organized and uploaded 2,000+ client success stories that you can watch for FREE today at: www.ThrivetimeShow.com/Testimonials.

I know the people in the success videos because I personally worked with them all in route to the achievement of their goals. I cannot be more sincere- if you will simply lock in to the concept of being coachable and putting in the work over the next 45 days, YOU TOO can become the next success story!

NOTABLE QUOTABLE

"As a personal trainer, I could spend hours telling you about great people like you who developed a NEVER QUIT MENTALITY as a result of finding a proven mentor and coaching program to help them to achieve massive success, but instead, I would like to conclude by focusing on you. I know that you can do it! I know that you can turn your fitness goals into reality. However, I know that in order to achieve your goals you must commit to taking action and to keep showing up for yourself, for your family and your future for the next 45 days!"

- COLTON CLAUSSEN
(The Founder of www.ClaussenTulsaPersonalTraining.com)

I sincerely believe that YOU have the mental capacity and tenacity needed to change for the better! My friend, my expectation is that this is going to be the BEST YEAR OF YOUR LIFE. Use the 45 day journal with a massive sense of urgency; and the ultimate achievement of your success will be inevitable. Always remember—what gets scheduled gets done.

- CLAY CLARK

Day 1 —F6 Goals for the Day:

What are your faith goals for today?	What time will you take action to achieve this goal?
What are your family goals for today?	What time will you take action to achieve this goal?
What are your financial goals for today?	What time will you take action to achieve this goal?
What are your fitness goals for today?	What time will you take action to achieve this goal?
What are your friendship goals for today?	What time will you take action to achieve this goal?
What are your fun goals for today?	What time will you take action to achieve this goal?
What are your nutrition goals for today?	What time are you going to eat today?

Day 2 —F6 Goals for the Day:

What are your faith goals for today?	**What time will you take action to achieve this goal?**
What are your family goals for today?	**What time will you take action to achieve this goal?**
What are your financial goals for today?	**What time will you take action to achieve this goal?**
What are your fitness goals for today?	**What time will you take action to achieve this goal?**
What are your friendship goals for today?	**What time will you take action to achieve this goal?**
What are your fun goals for today?	**What time will you take action to achieve this goal?**
What are your nutrition goals for today?	**What time are you going to eat today?**

Day 3 —F6 Goals for the Day:

What are your faith goals for today?	What time will you take action to achieve this goal?
What are your family goals for today?	What time will you take action to achieve this goal?
What are your financial goals for today?	What time will you take action to achieve this goal?
What are your fitness goals for today?	What time will you take action to achieve this goal?
What are your friendship goals for today?	What time will you take action to achieve this goal?
What are your fun goals for today?	What time will you take action to achieve this goal?
What are your nutrition goals for today?	What time are you going to eat today?

Day 4 —F6 Goals for the Day:

What are your faith goals for today?	What time will you take action to achieve this goal?
What are your family goals for today?	What time will you take action to achieve this goal?
What are your financial goals for today?	What time will you take action to achieve this goal?
What are your fitness goals for today?	What time will you take action to achieve this goal?
What are your friendship goals for today?	What time will you take action to achieve this goal?
What are your fun goals for today?	What time will you take action to achieve this goal?
What are your nutrition goals for today?	What time are you going to eat today?

Day 5 —F6 Goals for the Day:

What are your faith goals for today?	**What time will you take action to achieve this goal?**
What are your family goals for today?	**What time will you take action to achieve this goal?**
What are your financial goals for today?	**What time will you take action to achieve this goal?**
What are your fitness goals for today?	**What time will you take action to achieve this goal?**
What are your friendship goals for today?	**What time will you take action to achieve this goal?**
What are your fun goals for today?	**What time will you take action to achieve this goal?**
What are your nutrition goals for today?	**What time are you going to eat today?**

Day 6 —F6 Goals for the Day:

What are your faith goals for today?	**What time will you take action to achieve this goal?**
What are your family goals for today?	**What time will you take action to achieve this goal?**
What are your financial goals for today?	**What time will you take action to achieve this goal?**
What are your fitness goals for today?	**What time will you take action to achieve this goal?**
What are your friendship goals for today?	**What time will you take action to achieve this goal?**
What are your fun goals for today?	**What time will you take action to achieve this goal?**
What are your nutrition goals for today?	**What time are you going to eat today?**

Day 7 —F6 Goals for the Day:

What are your faith goals for today?	What time will you take action to achieve this goal?
What are your family goals for today?	What time will you take action to achieve this goal?
What are your financial goals for today?	What time will you take action to achieve this goal?
What are your fitness goals for today?	What time will you take action to achieve this goal?
What are your friendship goals for today?	What time will you take action to achieve this goal?
What are your fun goals for today?	What time will you take action to achieve this goal?
What are your nutrition goals for today?	What time are you going to eat today?

Day 8 —F6 Goals for the Day:

What are your faith goals for today?	**What time will you take action to achieve this goal?**
What are your family goals for today?	**What time will you take action to achieve this goal?**
What are your financial goals for today?	**What time will you take action to achieve this goal?**
What are your fitness goals for today?	**What time will you take action to achieve this goal?**
What are your friendship goals for today?	**What time will you take action to achieve this goal?**
What are your fun goals for today?	**What time will you take action to achieve this goal?**
What are your nutrition goals for today?	**What time are you going to eat today?**

Day 9 —F6 Goals for the Day:

What are your faith goals for today?	**What time will you take action to achieve this goal?**
What are your family goals for today?	**What time will you take action to achieve this goal?**
What are your financial goals for today?	**What time will you take action to achieve this goal?**
What are your fitness goals for today?	**What time will you take action to achieve this goal?**
What are your friendship goals for today?	**What time will you take action to achieve this goal?**
What are your fun goals for today?	**What time will you take action to achieve this goal?**
What are your nutrition goals for today?	**What time are you going to eat today?**

Day 10 —F6 Goals for the Day:

What are your faith goals for today?	What time will you take action to achieve this goal?
What are your family goals for today?	What time will you take action to achieve this goal?
What are your financial goals for today?	What time will you take action to achieve this goal?
What are your fitness goals for today?	What time will you take action to achieve this goal?
What are your friendship goals for today?	What time will you take action to achieve this goal?
What are your fun goals for today?	What time will you take action to achieve this goal?
What are your nutrition goals for today?	What time are you going to eat today?

Day 11 —F6 Goals for the Day:

What are your faith goals for today?	**What time will you take action to achieve this goal?**
What are your family goals for today?	**What time will you take action to achieve this goal?**
What are your financial goals for today?	**What time will you take action to achieve this goal?**
What are your fitness goals for today?	**What time will you take action to achieve this goal?**
What are your friendship goals for today?	**What time will you take action to achieve this goal?**
What are your fun goals for today?	**What time will you take action to achieve this goal?**
What are your nutrition goals for today?	**What time are you going to eat today?**

Day 12 —F6 Goals for the Day:

What are your faith goals for today?	**What time will you take action to achieve this goal?**
What are your family goals for today?	**What time will you take action to achieve this goal?**
What are your financial goals for today?	**What time will you take action to achieve this goal?**
What are your fitness goals for today?	**What time will you take action to achieve this goal?**
What are your friendship goals for today?	**What time will you take action to achieve this goal?**
What are your fun goals for today?	**What time will you take action to achieve this goal?**
What are your nutrition goals for today?	**What time are you going to eat today?**

Day 13 —F6 Goals for the Day:

What are your faith goals for today?	What time will you take action to achieve this goal?
What are your family goals for today?	What time will you take action to achieve this goal?
What are your financial goals for today?	What time will you take action to achieve this goal?
What are your fitness goals for today?	What time will you take action to achieve this goal?
What are your friendship goals for today?	What time will you take action to achieve this goal?
What are your fun goals for today?	What time will you take action to achieve this goal?
What are your nutrition goals for today?	What time are you going to eat today?

Day 14 —F6 Goals for the Day:

What are your faith goals for today?	**What time will you take action to achieve this goal?**
What are your family goals for today?	**What time will you take action to achieve this goal?**
What are your financial goals for today?	**What time will you take action to achieve this goal?**
What are your fitness goals for today?	**What time will you take action to achieve this goal?**
What are your friendship goals for today?	**What time will you take action to achieve this goal?**
What are your fun goals for today?	**What time will you take action to achieve this goal?**
What are your nutrition goals for today?	**What time are you going to eat today?**

Day 15 —F6 Goals for the Day:

What are your faith goals for today?	What time will you take action to achieve this goal?
What are your family goals for today?	What time will you take action to achieve this goal?
What are your financial goals for today?	What time will you take action to achieve this goal?
What are your fitness goals for today?	What time will you take action to achieve this goal?
What are your friendship goals for today?	What time will you take action to achieve this goal?
What are your fun goals for today?	What time will you take action to achieve this goal?
What are your nutrition goals for today?	What time are you going to eat today?

Day 16 —F6 Goals for the Day:

What are your faith goals for today?	**What time will you take action to achieve this goal?**
What are your family goals for today?	**What time will you take action to achieve this goal?**
What are your financial goals for today?	**What time will you take action to achieve this goal?**
What are your fitness goals for today?	**What time will you take action to achieve this goal?**
What are your friendship goals for today?	**What time will you take action to achieve this goal?**
What are your fun goals for today?	**What time will you take action to achieve this goal?**
What are your nutrition goals for today?	**What time are you going to eat today?**

Day 17 —F6 Goals for the Day:

What are your faith goals for today?	**What time will you take action to achieve this goal?**
What are your family goals for today?	**What time will you take action to achieve this goal?**
What are your financial goals for today?	**What time will you take action to achieve this goal?**
What are your fitness goals for today?	**What time will you take action to achieve this goal?**
What are your friendship goals for today?	**What time will you take action to achieve this goal?**
What are your fun goals for today?	**What time will you take action to achieve this goal?**
What are your nutrition goals for today?	**What time are you going to eat today?**

Day 18 —F6 Goals for the Day:

What are your faith goals for today?	**What time will you take action to achieve this goal?**
What are your family goals for today?	**What time will you take action to achieve this goal?**
What are your financial goals for today?	**What time will you take action to achieve this goal?**
What are your fitness goals for today?	**What time will you take action to achieve this goal?**
What are your friendship goals for today?	**What time will you take action to achieve this goal?**
What are your fun goals for today?	**What time will you take action to achieve this goal?**
What are your nutrition goals for today?	**What time are you going to eat today?**

Day 19 — F6 Goals for the Day:

What are your faith goals for today?	What time will you take action to achieve this goal?
What are your family goals for today?	What time will you take action to achieve this goal?
What are your financial goals for today?	What time will you take action to achieve this goal?
What are your fitness goals for today?	What time will you take action to achieve this goal?
What are your friendship goals for today?	What time will you take action to achieve this goal?
What are your fun goals for today?	What time will you take action to achieve this goal?
What are your nutrition goals for today?	What time are you going to eat today?

Day 20 —F6 Goals for the Day:

What are your faith goals for today?	**What time will you take action to achieve this goal?**
What are your family goals for today?	**What time will you take action to achieve this goal?**
What are your financial goals for today?	**What time will you take action to achieve this goal?**
What are your fitness goals for today?	**What time will you take action to achieve this goal?**
What are your friendship goals for today?	**What time will you take action to achieve this goal?**
What are your fun goals for today?	**What time will you take action to achieve this goal?**
What are your nutrition goals for today?	**What time are you going to eat today?**

Day 21 —F6 Goals for the Day:

What are your faith goals for today?	**What time will you take action to achieve this goal?**
What are your family goals for today?	**What time will you take action to achieve this goal?**
What are your financial goals for today?	**What time will you take action to achieve this goal?**
What are your fitness goals for today?	**What time will you take action to achieve this goal?**
What are your friendship goals for today?	**What time will you take action to achieve this goal?**
What are your fun goals for today?	**What time will you take action to achieve this goal?**
What are your nutrition goals for today?	**What time are you going to eat today?**

Day 22 —F6 Goals for the Day:

What are your faith goals for today?	**What time will you take action to achieve this goal?**
What are your family goals for today?	**What time will you take action to achieve this goal?**
What are your financial goals for today?	**What time will you take action to achieve this goal?**
What are your fitness goals for today?	**What time will you take action to achieve this goal?**
What are your friendship goals for today?	**What time will you take action to achieve this goal?**
What are your fun goals for today?	**What time will you take action to achieve this goal?**
What are your nutrition goals for today?	**What time are you going to eat today?**

Day 23 —F6 Goals for the Day:

What are your faith goals for today?	What time will you take action to achieve this goal?
What are your family goals for today?	What time will you take action to achieve this goal?
What are your financial goals for today?	What time will you take action to achieve this goal?
What are your fitness goals for today?	What time will you take action to achieve this goal?
What are your friendship goals for today?	What time will you take action to achieve this goal?
What are your fun goals for today?	What time will you take action to achieve this goal?
What are your nutrition goals for today?	What time are you going to eat today?

Day 24 —F6 Goals for the Day:

What are your faith goals for today?	**What time will you take action to achieve this goal?**
What are your family goals for today?	**What time will you take action to achieve this goal?**
What are your financial goals for today?	**What time will you take action to achieve this goal?**
What are your fitness goals for today?	**What time will you take action to achieve this goal?**
What are your friendship goals for today?	**What time will you take action to achieve this goal?**
What are your fun goals for today?	**What time will you take action to achieve this goal?**
What are your nutrition goals for today?	**What time are you going to eat today?**

Day 25 —F6 Goals for the Day:

What are your faith goals for today?	What time will you take action to achieve this goal?
What are your family goals for today?	What time will you take action to achieve this goal?
What are your financial goals for today?	What time will you take action to achieve this goal?
What are your fitness goals for today?	What time will you take action to achieve this goal?
What are your friendship goals for today?	What time will you take action to achieve this goal?
What are your fun goals for today?	What time will you take action to achieve this goal?
What are your nutrition goals for today?	What time are you going to eat today?

Day 26 —F6 Goals for the Day:

What are your faith goals for today?	**What time will you take action to achieve this goal?**
What are your family goals for today?	**What time will you take action to achieve this goal?**
What are your financial goals for today?	**What time will you take action to achieve this goal?**
What are your fitness goals for today?	**What time will you take action to achieve this goal?**
What are your friendship goals for today?	**What time will you take action to achieve this goal?**
What are your fun goals for today?	**What time will you take action to achieve this goal?**
What are your nutrition goals for today?	**What time are you going to eat today?**

Day 27 —F6 Goals for the Day:

What are your faith goals for today?	**What time will you take action to achieve this goal?**
What are your family goals for today?	**What time will you take action to achieve this goal?**
What are your financial goals for today?	**What time will you take action to achieve this goal?**
What are your fitness goals for today?	**What time will you take action to achieve this goal?**
What are your friendship goals for today?	**What time will you take action to achieve this goal?**
What are your fun goals for today?	**What time will you take action to achieve this goal?**
What are your nutrition goals for today?	**What time are you going to eat today?**

Day 28 —F6 Goals for the Day:

What are your faith goals for today?	**What time will you take action to achieve this goal?**
What are your family goals for today?	**What time will you take action to achieve this goal?**
What are your financial goals for today?	**What time will you take action to achieve this goal?**
What are your fitness goals for today?	**What time will you take action to achieve this goal?**
What are your friendship goals for today?	**What time will you take action to achieve this goal?**
What are your fun goals for today?	**What time will you take action to achieve this goal?**
What are your nutrition goals for today?	**What time are you going to eat today?**

Day 29 —F6 Goals for the Day:

What are your faith goals for today?	**What time will you take action to achieve this goal?**
What are your family goals for today?	**What time will you take action to achieve this goal?**
What are your financial goals for today?	**What time will you take action to achieve this goal?**
What are your fitness goals for today?	**What time will you take action to achieve this goal?**
What are your friendship goals for today?	**What time will you take action to achieve this goal?**
What are your fun goals for today?	**What time will you take action to achieve this goal?**
What are your nutrition goals for today?	**What time are you going to eat today?**

Day 30 —F6 Goals for the Day:

What are your faith goals for today?	What time will you take action to achieve this goal?
What are your family goals for today?	What time will you take action to achieve this goal?
What are your financial goals for today?	What time will you take action to achieve this goal?
What are your fitness goals for today?	What time will you take action to achieve this goal?
What are your friendship goals for today?	What time will you take action to achieve this goal?
What are your fun goals for today?	What time will you take action to achieve this goal?
What are your nutrition goals for today?	What time are you going to eat today?

Day 31 —F6 Goals for the Day:

What are your faith goals for today?	**What time will you take action to achieve this goal?**
What are your family goals for today?	**What time will you take action to achieve this goal?**
What are your financial goals for today?	**What time will you take action to achieve this goal?**
What are your fitness goals for today?	**What time will you take action to achieve this goal?**
What are your friendship goals for today?	**What time will you take action to achieve this goal?**
What are your fun goals for today?	**What time will you take action to achieve this goal?**
What are your nutrition goals for today?	**What time are you going to eat today?**

Day 32 —F6 Goals for the Day:

What are your faith goals for today?	**What time will you take action to achieve this goal?**
What are your family goals for today?	**What time will you take action to achieve this goal?**
What are your financial goals for today?	**What time will you take action to achieve this goal?**
What are your fitness goals for today?	**What time will you take action to achieve this goal?**
What are your friendship goals for today?	**What time will you take action to achieve this goal?**
What are your fun goals for today?	**What time will you take action to achieve this goal?**
What are your nutrition goals for today?	**What time are you going to eat today?**

Day 33 —F6 Goals for the Day:

What are your faith goals for today?	**What time will you take action to achieve this goal?**
What are your family goals for today?	**What time will you take action to achieve this goal?**
What are your financial goals for today?	**What time will you take action to achieve this goal?**
What are your fitness goals for today?	**What time will you take action to achieve this goal?**
What are your friendship goals for today?	**What time will you take action to achieve this goal?**
What are your fun goals for today?	**What time will you take action to achieve this goal?**
What are your nutrition goals for today?	**What time are you going to eat today?**

Day 34 —F6 Goals for the Day:

What are your faith goals for today?	What time will you take action to achieve this goal?
What are your family goals for today?	What time will you take action to achieve this goal?
What are your financial goals for today?	What time will you take action to achieve this goal?
What are your fitness goals for today?	What time will you take action to achieve this goal?
What are your friendship goals for today?	What time will you take action to achieve this goal?
What are your fun goals for today?	What time will you take action to achieve this goal?
What are your nutrition goals for today?	What time are you going to eat today?

Day 35 —F6 Goals for the Day:

What are your faith goals for today?	What time will you take action to achieve this goal?
What are your family goals for today?	What time will you take action to achieve this goal?
What are your financial goals for today?	What time will you take action to achieve this goal?
What are your fitness goals for today?	What time will you take action to achieve this goal?
What are your friendship goals for today?	What time will you take action to achieve this goal?
What are your fun goals for today?	What time will you take action to achieve this goal?
What are your nutrition goals for today?	What time are you going to eat today?

Day 36 —F6 Goals for the Day:

What are your faith goals for today?	What time will you take action to achieve this goal?
What are your family goals for today?	What time will you take action to achieve this goal?
What are your financial goals for today?	What time will you take action to achieve this goal?
What are your fitness goals for today?	What time will you take action to achieve this goal?
What are your friendship goals for today?	What time will you take action to achieve this goal?
What are your fun goals for today?	What time will you take action to achieve this goal?
What are your nutrition goals for today?	What time are you going to eat today?

Day 37 —F6 Goals for the Day:

What are your faith goals for today?	**What time will you take action to achieve this goal?**
What are your family goals for today?	**What time will you take action to achieve this goal?**
What are your financial goals for today?	**What time will you take action to achieve this goal?**
What are your fitness goals for today?	**What time will you take action to achieve this goal?**
What are your friendship goals for today?	**What time will you take action to achieve this goal?**
What are your fun goals for today?	**What time will you take action to achieve this goal?**
What are your nutrition goals for today?	**What time are you going to eat today?**

Day 38 —F6 Goals for the Day:

What are your faith goals for today?	**What time will you take action to achieve this goal?**
What are your family goals for today?	**What time will you take action to achieve this goal?**
What are your financial goals for today?	**What time will you take action to achieve this goal?**
What are your fitness goals for today?	**What time will you take action to achieve this goal?**
What are your friendship goals for today?	**What time will you take action to achieve this goal?**
What are your fun goals for today?	**What time will you take action to achieve this goal?**
What are your nutrition goals for today?	**What time are you going to eat today?**

Day 39 —F6 Goals for the Day:

What are your faith goals for today?	What time will you take action to achieve this goal?
What are your family goals for today?	What time will you take action to achieve this goal?
What are your financial goals for today?	What time will you take action to achieve this goal?
What are your fitness goals for today?	What time will you take action to achieve this goal?
What are your friendship goals for today?	What time will you take action to achieve this goal?
What are your fun goals for today?	What time will you take action to achieve this goal?
What are your nutrition goals for today?	What time are you going to eat today?

Day 40 —F6 Goals for the Day:

What are your faith goals for today?	**What time will you take action to achieve this goal?**
What are your family goals for today?	**What time will you take action to achieve this goal?**
What are your financial goals for today?	**What time will you take action to achieve this goal?**
What are your fitness goals for today?	**What time will you take action to achieve this goal?**
What are your friendship goals for today?	**What time will you take action to achieve this goal?**
What are your fun goals for today?	**What time will you take action to achieve this goal?**
What are your nutrition goals for today?	**What time are you going to eat today?**

Day 41 —F6 Goals for the Day:

What are your faith goals for today?	**What time will you take action to achieve this goal?**
What are your family goals for today?	**What time will you take action to achieve this goal?**
What are your financial goals for today?	**What time will you take action to achieve this goal?**
What are your fitness goals for today?	**What time will you take action to achieve this goal?**
What are your friendship goals for today?	**What time will you take action to achieve this goal?**
What are your fun goals for today?	**What time will you take action to achieve this goal?**
What are your nutrition goals for today?	**What time are you going to eat today?**

Day 42 —F6 Goals for the Day:

What are your faith goals for today?	What time will you take action to achieve this goal?
What are your family goals for today?	What time will you take action to achieve this goal?
What are your financial goals for today?	What time will you take action to achieve this goal?
What are your fitness goals for today?	What time will you take action to achieve this goal?
What are your friendship goals for today?	What time will you take action to achieve this goal?
What are your fun goals for today?	What time will you take action to achieve this goal?
What are your nutrition goals for today?	What time are you going to eat today?

Day 43 —F6 Goals for the Day:

What are your faith goals for today?	What time will you take action to achieve this goal?
What are your family goals for today?	What time will you take action to achieve this goal?
What are your financial goals for today?	What time will you take action to achieve this goal?
What are your fitness goals for today?	What time will you take action to achieve this goal?
What are your friendship goals for today?	What time will you take action to achieve this goal?
What are your fun goals for today?	What time will you take action to achieve this goal?
What are your nutrition goals for today?	What time are you going to eat today?

Day 44 —F6 Goals for the Day:

What are your faith goals for today?	**What time will you take action to achieve this goal?**
What are your family goals for today?	**What time will you take action to achieve this goal?**
What are your financial goals for today?	**What time will you take action to achieve this goal?**
What are your fitness goals for today?	**What time will you take action to achieve this goal?**
What are your friendship goals for today?	**What time will you take action to achieve this goal?**
What are your fun goals for today?	**What time will you take action to achieve this goal?**
What are your nutrition goals for today?	**What time are you going to eat today?**

Day 45 —F6 Goals for the Day:

What are your faith goals for today?	What time will you take action to achieve this goal?
What are your family goals for today?	What time will you take action to achieve this goal?
What are your financial goals for today?	What time will you take action to achieve this goal?
What are your fitness goals for today?	What time will you take action to achieve this goal?
What are your friendship goals for today?	What time will you take action to achieve this goal?
What are your fun goals for today?	What time will you take action to achieve this goal?
What are your nutrition goals for today?	What time are you going to eat today?

www.ingramcontent.com/pod-product-compliance
Lightning Source LLC
Jackson TN
JSHW032035110426
100734JS00005B/20